A REVIEW

OF THE

CRIMEAN WAR.

A REVIEW

OF THE

CRIMEAN WAR,

TO THE WINTER OF 1854-5.

BY

LIEUT.-COLONEL JOHN ADYE, C.B.,

LATE ASSISTANT ADJUTANT-GENERAL, ROYAL ARTILLERY.

With a new introduction by

Colonel John F. Adye, D.S.O.

Si vis pacem, para bellum.

The long preparation required for any military enterprise, is the chief difficulty in the art of war.—*Times*, December, 1855.

EP Publishing Limited

1973

INTRODUCTION

by Colonel John F. Adye, D.S.O. (retired)

My grandfather wrote a most readable account of the Crimean War to the winter of 1854–55. His loyalty to the Commander-in-Chief, General (later Field Marshal) Lord Raglan, permeates throughout the work, and is evidenced by the fact of his castigation of *The Times* newspaper (see page 5).

The book records on pages 5 and 6 the numbers of men and staff required to carry out an expedition of this sort, but which were not sent out by the Government of the day.

It records the siege of Silistria and the journey to the Crimean Peninsular.

It records the Battle of the Alma in September 1854.

It records the first bombardment of Sebastopol, on 17th October 1854.

It records the Battle of Balaclava on 25th October 1854.

It records the Battle of Inkerman on 5th November 1854.

Throughout it gives the number of casualties sustained in the above Battles.

It records the death of Brig. General T. Fox-Strangways on pages 132 and 133 and how he and the C-in-C had fought at Leipsic and Waterloo; in my grandfather's autobiography *Recollection of a Military Life* published in 1895 by Smith Elder & Co., on pages 59 and 60, he records one of his last words were: "Take me to the gunners, let me die amongst the gunners".

From the book *The History of the Royal Artillery (Crimean Period)* by Colonel Julian R. J. Jocelyn, published in 1911 by John Murray, are taken the numbers of the Artillery Batteries and Companies taking part in the Crimean War 1854–55, with their commanding Officers' names—Cavalry Brigade.

I Troop RHA (now "O" Bty. RHA) Captain G. A. Maude, RHA

First Division, Lieut. Colonel R. J. Dacres, R.A.

"A" Battery (now 38 Bty. RFA) Captain D. W. Paynter, R.A.

"H" Battery (now 64 Bty. RFA) Captain E. Wodehouse, R.A.

Second Division, Lieut. Colonel R. J. Fitzmayer, R.A.

"B" Battery (now 14 Bty. RFA) Captain C. T. Franklin, R.A.

"G" Battery (now 19 Bty. RFA) Captain J. Turner, R.A.

Third Division, Lieut. Colonel R. J. Dupuis, R.A.

"F" Battery (now 7 Bty. RFA) Captain W. Swinton, R.A.

"W" Battery (now 62 Bty. RFA) Captain G. R. Barker, R.A.

Fourth Division (in Reserve)

"P" Battery (now 63 Bty. RFA) Brevet Major S. P. Townsend, R.A.

Light Division, Lieut. Colonel N. T. Lake, R.A.

"C" Troop (now "C" Bty. RHA) Captain J. J. Brandwing, R.A.

"E" Battery (now 12 Bty. RFA) Captain J. R. Anderson, R.A.

Siege Train, Lieut. Colonel G. Gambier, R.A.

Right Attack, 11 Battalion Nos. 1, 6, 7, 8 Companies, Brevet Lieut. Colonel C. Dickson.

Left Attack, 12 Battalion Nos. 2, 3, 6, 7 Companies, Brevet Major A. Irving, R.G.A.

The above were the Officers commanding at the Battle of The Alma, September 1854, and the Batteries in brackets refer to the numbers of the Batteries when the book was written in 1911.

It is interesting to note that Captain Brevet Major J. M. Adye was granted the rank of Lieut. Colonel and the C.B. as a result of this campaign; that in 1874 he was commandant of the Royal Military Academy at Woolwich; that in 1882 he was Chief of Staff to General Sir Garnet Wolseley at Tel-El-Kebir; that on 1st January 1883 he was appointed Governor and Commander-in-Chief Gibraltar.

Introduction

My father Major General Sir John Adye, K.C.M.G., C.B., never served in the substantive rank of Captain as he was appointed Brevet Major after the battle of Tel-El-Kebir, 1882, where he was A.D.C. to C-in-C General Wolseley.

My father wrote his autobiography, published by Herbert Jenkins Ltd. in 1925, *Soldiers and Others I have Known*, and also *Napoleon of the Snows*, published by Nash & Grayson in 1931.

I claim that the Adye family is the longest serving (since 1757) and the most numerous (nine members) in the Royal Regiment of Artillery.

The United Service & Royal Aero Club,
Pall Mall,
London, S.W.1.
10th March 1973.

PREFACE.

THE following notes, relative to the Crimean War, were written chiefly in 1857, with a view to publication, but owing to my having been suddenly ordered from England for service in India, they were necessarily laid aside for the time.

I had hoped that a return home would, by giving me access to official documents, and other means or references not available in this country, have enabled me to render my narrative more full and complete.

My official duties, however, detain me in India, and I have, accordingly, decided on publishing my notes as they are, believing that, although they afford but an imperfect sketch of the events of the Crimean Campaign, they still give correct information on many points hitherto much misrepresented.

JOHN ADYE,
LIEUT.-COLONEL, R. A.

Madras,
November, 1859.

CONTENTS.

CHAPTER I.

CHAPTER II.

CHAPTER III.

CHAPTER IV.

CHAPTER V.

CHAPTER VI.

CHAPTER VII.

CHAPTER XI.

CHAPTER XII.

CHAPTER XIII.

CHAPTER XIV.

A REVIEW

OF

THE CRIMEAN WAR.

CHAPTER I.

THE late war, at its commencement, found England unprepared, and its people, as a general rule, ignorant of the requirements and previous preparation which war entails. The available army was small, and all the various departments which contribute to its efficiency, and are of vital importance in taking the field, either did not exist at all, or were incomplete, reduced, and consequently inefficient. It is unnecessary now to enter into the question as to whom blame is to be attributed for such a state of things. The relaxing effects of a 40 years' peace had increased the ordinary indifference of the nation, as regards military arrangements. The insular position of England renders unnecessary the maintenance, for her own safety, of a large standing army, such as is of vital necessity with the other nations of Europe;

1

but it follows also that in the event of a general war, she has no force which either in numbers or efficiency for the field can compare with those of the great continental powers, or can enable her to take any other than a subordinate part in the struggle. The requirements and establishments of a force kept up simply with the view to a country's defence are of a very modified nature as compared with those of an army intended for distant and active operations in an enemy's country. An army cannot be improvised; although men, materials, and money may be forthcoming, time and study are required to render it fit to take the field.

Before entering into any account of the late war, and more particularly of the contests in which the British were engaged, it will be useful and interesting to consider for a few moments the composition and requirements of an army, and how far that of England in 1854 fulfilled any of the conditions requisite to success.

To commence with men. The army which a nation sends into the field ought to bear, in point of numbers, but a small proportion to the actual force it has to maintain under arms. The reasons are obvious. An army on active service is always unhealthy, and its ranks are constantly diminishing. Sickness invariably follows it in a greater or less degree. Insufficient shelter, bad food, irregular hours, hard work, and undue crowding, may account for this fact. When the casualties of actual warfare are added, there will be no difficulty in understanding the rapid diminution of the effective of an army in the field, and the necessity therefore of large reserves to recruit its ranks.

A few facts, gathered from the experience of the Crimean war, will render the appreciation of this more simple. During the first year the casualties of the English army amounted to an average of nearly 3000 men per month (36,000 per annum). Again, after two years' war we had actually buried upwards of 21,000 men,—being rather more than the original number sent to the East; and the French and Russians, it is said, suffered even in greater proportion. It may be argued that this is an exaggerated and exceptional case; the army having suffered, first from cholera and fever at Varna, then by severe actions in the field, succeeded by the hardships and almost starvation of the winter of 1854-55. This may be true, but its very excesses will enable us to form an opinion of the necessity of large reserves. It may therefore be concluded, that in order to keep an army of 20,000 men on active service, double that number should be held in readiness at home, disciplined and ready to replace casualties.

Another point of importance is the education of an army. Mere numbers do not alone consti-

tute strength; self-reliance, the harmony of its
component parts, and above all the efficiency of
its administrative branches, such as the General
Staff, the Commissariat, and the Medical Departments, &c., can only be obtained by study, practical experience, and by the periodical assembly
of troops in camp. And when an army takes
the field, a fresh source of difficulty displays
itself, viz.: its means of moving. However well
organized it may be in other respects, however
anxious to meet the enemy,—if it fail in mobility
it fails in one of the most important elements of
success. The Commander-in-Chief must be con-
tinually frustrated in his plans, and must often
labour under the disadvantage of leaving to his
enemy the choice of ground for combat, and of
being unable to follow up a victory. It is impossible to exaggerate the importance of efficiency
in this branch of an army's equipment.

The following remarks bearing on the subject
of our army administration at the outset of the
war are interesting :—

"More is done towards the success of wars
and the triumph of policy by military administration, than by diplomacy in the Cabinet or by
courage in the field." Again—"We intend to
convey no aspersion on any member of the present or of any former Government, when we say
that those great studies of the art by which
armies are raised, transported, and fed,—by which,

in short, war is carried on, have but seldom engrossed the thoughts of the statesmen of this country. And if 40 years of peace have left us almost without experience of former wars, and have recently taken from us alone the last of the giants of those days, it is the more incumbent on us to leave nothing undone which reason or foresight suggest to enable our armies to support their ancient renown."

These words, so true in their argument, are extracted from the Times of April, 1854; and it is only extraordinary that a paper, possessing so accurate a knowledge of the theory and art of war, and knowing the unfit condition of the English army at the time, should afterwards have advocated at all hazards the expedition to the Crimea. It is still more extraordinary that in the winter of 1854, when the British army became overwhelmed with difficulties, this paper should have attributed to the officers in charge the misfortunes which alone arose from the nation's neglect.

It would therefore appear that in order to maintain an army of say 20,000 men in the field, the following are some of the more important requisites:

20,000 men ....   In the field.

20,000 men ....   { Trained soldiers ready to take the field .... } 1st Reserve.

20,000 men ....   Under training .... 2nd Reserve.

General Staff...
Medical Staff ..
Commissariat Staff
{ To consist of officers carefully selected, educated, and accustomed to the duties entailed by the concentration of troops.

Transport for the conveyance of ....
{ Food for the army.
Reserve ammunition for infantry, cavalry, and artillery.
Camp equipage.
Baggage.
Medical stores, and the sick and wounded.
Pontoon train.
Engineer's stores, &c. &c.
Siege train.

Now what was the state of the British army sent to the East in 1854 ?

One may almost put the pen through every item except the first. When the 20,000 men had left England, the country was almost drained of its soldiers ; of reserves, consequently, there were next to none.

The report of the Committee of the House of Commons on the " State of the Army before Sebastopol " thus speaks of this question: " At the date of the expedition to the East, no reserve was provided at home adequate to the undertaking. Mr. Sidney Herbert states in his memorandum of the 27th November,—The army in the East has been created by discounting the future; every regiment at home, or within reach, and not forming part of the army, has been robbed to complete it. The depôts of battalions under Lord Raglan have been similarly treated." And, as an army, even this number was uneducated.

With the exception of the trifling experiment at Chobham, the troops had never been assembled in masses. As far as manly strength, perfect discipline, willing obedience, and high courage availed, the regiments might individually be considered as superior to those of any nation perhaps in the world. But the mere collection of regiments on the outbreak of war does not compose an army. Again : omitting some of the general and higher officers, few of the staff had ever had an opportunity of seeing an English force assembled in the field.* With regard to the medical department, skilful as the officers might be in a strictly professional point of view, what chance had they ever had of acquiring administrative knowledge of the requirements of a large army ? The head of the commissariat (Mr. Filder) was an officer who had only held a subordinate position in the war of 40 years before, and the state of his department may be gathered from the following extract of his own remarks : "None of the subordinate establishments absolutely necessary to the efficiency of a field commissariat existed at the outbreak of the war, and even the officers had to be collected from the most distant

* The French are very particular in the education of their staff. Every officer, prior to entering it, has to serve two years in each of the three branches of the service, infantry, artillery, and cavalry ; they are then placed permanently on the staff. Although this system may, by removing officers altogether from active regimental duties, tend to incline them to routine and theory, still such training, if not perfect, must possess many advantages.

parts of the empire; from Sierra Leone, the Cape of Good Hope, and New South Wales, and, of course, by slow degrees. In the mean time, I had to carry on the duties with the temporary assistance of gentlemen furnished from other public departments, and wholly without experience in commissariat service. This inefficient state of the department, when I took charge of it, necessarily diverted much of my attention from the more important general arrangements of the service, to the regulation of details; but I notice it less for the purpose of accounting for my own possible errors and omissions, than with the object of meeting the comparison which has been frequently made elsewhere, and is partially made use of in this report, between the success of the British and French commissariat operations. That the success has been uniformly on the side of the former is far from being established; but that generally it ought to be so, is quite clear, inasmuch as there is the greatest possible advantage on that side in the completeness of the establishments on which so much of commissariat success depends. These are not, as with us, discarded at the termination of a period of active warfare, and wholly neglected during the continuance of peace, but are constantly kept up in an effective, even if a reduced, state, and are considered as necessary an accompaniment of every body of detached troops, as any other portion of the army; and thus give a facility of action to a French force at the outset, which can be acquired by an English army only after long and perhaps disastrous as well as costly experience. I do not presume here to enter into the question whether or not a similar system ought to be adopted in our service; but the fact that no such system does exist in it should be taken into consideration in estimating the exertions of the British commissariat officers, who usually, like myself, are thrown at once upon their own slightly aided resources, and compelled to occupy themselves in creating the means of action at the moment when action is already needed."

As to transport, or any means of moving the impediments, provisions, or ammunition, nothing of the kind existed! The army, such as it was, was perfectly immoveable.

Now if such as I have stated was the condition of the English force in 1854, did it carry the elements of success with it? Small as were its numbers, did they even represent efficiency in proportion to their front? In entering into a war, then, against an antagonist whose armies numbered hundreds of thousands, and in company with an ally whose force was almost as powerful, and with both of whom war had been a constant study and a matter of preparation, we could only hope, so far as our land force was concerned, to take a subordinate position; more especially must this have been the case in the totally unprepared condition of our small army for active operations.

But these were by no means the feelings with which England commenced the war; consequently, we suffered mortification, as our deficiencies became apparent, and still more so towards the close, in finding that the great proportions of the struggle no longer remained in our hands; we spent millions in resuscitating defunct establishments, and in raising new and temporary ones; but all were too late to save the army from intense suffering, and the country from reproach and from loss of caste among the military nations of Europe.

CHAPTER II.

When the allied armies arrived in the East, the position of affairs was critical. The Russians were upon the Danube, and, once across this great impediment, no line of defence remained, except the range of the Balkan Mountains. There is a very clever letter written by " An English Officer," and entitled " A strategic view of the War on the Danube," which, although it appeared as far back as January, 1854, before war was declared, gives so clear an account of the military position of Turkey in this direction, that I have extracted some sentences :—

"The Balkan is the main line of defence of Turkey : the Danube forms an immense wet ditch in its front, strengthened by the strong outworks of Hirsova, Silistria, Rustshuk, and Widdin; and the plain of Bulgaria a vast glacis between the two. The entrenched camp of Shumla, situated in the northern spurs of the Balkan, where they melt into the Bulgarian plains, is a position of the greatest strength and importance, flanking the whole eastern part of the

main line. In attacking this position the Russians
must assail either its right, its centre, or its left. To
attack its right their armies must force the passage
of the lower Danube, capture some of the fortresses
on that river to secure their communications, and then
advance by Bayarik. They would then have the
Black Sea, held by the united squadrons, on their left
flank; the strong fortresses of Shumla and Varna in
their front; Silistria (if not previously reduced, and it
would, if well defended, require a long siege) in rear
of their right; and the main Turkish army concentrated round Shumla, ready to operate against their
right flank and communications in the plain between
that point and the Danube. Now, to take Varna
when supported by the allied squadrons, would be extremely difficult; to force Shumla, if the Turkish
forces were well handled, far more so; and to advance
without the reduction of one or two of these places,
an impossibility. Even supposing Varna fell, as long
as the allied fleets held the Black Sea on the one side,
and the Turks Shumla on the other, no advance could
be made. Now, the excessive strength of Shumla,
the result of the campaigns of 1812, 1828, and 1829
has clearly demonstrated. The right of the line may
therefore be looked upon as secure. Again: in the
event of the Russians forcing the line of the Danube,
and moving on Sophia, the great object of the Turkish
commanders should be to hold their army concentrated in the plain of Bulgaria; carefully to avoid a general action in the field (where the inferiority of their

infantry in discipline and of their cavalry in numbers to the Russians, would certainly lead to defeat); to preserve their communications with Shumla, and, by means of demonstrations along the Danube, to threaten the long line of the Russian communications through Wallachia. This would be effected by, in military phrase, refusing their left and centre, and operating offensively on the Danube with their right. As long as Omar Pasha holds the fortresses of Rustshuk and Silistria on the Danube, and points all his operations on Shumla, the Russian advances will be arrested, unless a decisive victory in the field gives them the entire command of Bulgaria."

In order to follow the progress of events, after the arrival of the allies in Turkey, and to understand their gradual change of tactics from those of defence to an aggressive movement against a part of the Russian Empire, I have made some further extracts from documents which are either official, or partake of that character. The following from the instructions of the Emperor Napoleon to Marshal St. Arnaud, dated the 12th April, 1854, explain clearly the views then entertained, and the reasons for sending the armies to Varna :—

" The Anglo-French army once united on the shores of the Sea of Marmora, you must concert measures with Omar Pasha and Lord Raglan for the adoption of one of three following plans.

" 1. Either to advance to meet the Russians in the Balkans.

" 2. Or to seize upon the Crimea.

" 3. Or to land at Odessa, or any other part of the Russian coast of the Black Sea.

" In the first case, Varna appears to me the most important point to be occupied; the infantry might be taken there by sea, and the cavalry more easily perhaps by land. On no account ought the army to go too far from the Black Sea, so as to be always in free communication with the fleets.

" In the second case,—that of the occupation of the Crimea,—the place of landing must first be made sure of, that it may take place at a distance from the enemy, and that it may be speedily fortified, so as to serve as a *point d'appui* to fall back upon in case of a retreat. The capture of Sebastopol must not be attempted without at least half a siege train, and a great number of sacks of earth. When within reach of the place, do not omit seizing upon Balaclava, a little port situated about four leagues south of Sebastopol, and by means of which easy communication may be kept up with the fleet during the siege.

The Moniteur, the French official paper, in an article published afterwards, explained the further progress of events as follows :—

" But scarcely had the Anglo-French army arrived at Gallipoli, when the scene changed. Although the Russian skirmishes had been seen from Varna, the heroic defence of Silistria had stopped the advance of Prince Gortschakoff: the struggle instead of being carried on in the heart of the Empire, was prolonged on the Danube with varied chances of success. The commanders of the expedition then thought they would have time to reach the theatre of the struggle, and perhaps to save Silistria; but at all events to join the Ottoman army, and to defend the Balkans against the Russians, having their wings, so to say, protected by the fortresses of Shumla and Varna. This plan was as bold as it was prudent. It was indicated moreover by circumstances, and by the imminence of the danger. If, indeed, the Russians had taken Silistria, the fall of which was announced as inevitable by Omar Pasha's reports, the fall of the Ottoman Empire might depend on a great battle. It was requisite for the armies of France and England to be prepared for it; there was their post, because there perhaps the struggle would be decided, and the supreme decrees of fate fulfilled. Events did not realize these previsions. The courage of the Turkish army and the presence of the allies sufficed to make the Russians raise the siege, and withdraw to the other side of the Danube.

" Whenever an enemy retires, it offers a great temptation to the army before which it retires; namely, to pursue. But when such pursuit may compromise an army, there is more glory in remaining still than in advancing. The love of glory must never outstrip the biddings of wisdom. What could the Anglo-French army have done by entering a devastated country, without roads, inundated by water, and infected with pestilential diseases? They would have found, not victory, but destruction without a struggle, death without a compensation.

"But what could the united Generals do at Varna after the retreat of the Russian army? Were they to remain in inactivity, which would have led to discouragement, and from which the prestige of our flag would have inevitably suffered? Neither military honour nor political interest allowed the Commander-in-Chief to take such a position. Once in this great theatre, inaction was out of the question; it was necessary to act, to show an object to the troops; to compel the enemy to fear us; to excite the ambition of Europe to follow us, by arousing its admiration and respect. It was then only that a landing in the Crimea was mooted. An expedition against Sebastopol might hasten the denouement of the war. It had a determined and limited object; it might place in the hands of the allies a province and a stronghold which, once conquered, would be a pledge and a means of exchange to obtain peace.

"It was under the influence of these considerations that the Commanders-in-Chief conceived the idea, and decreed the execution, of this plan. The expedition having been examined, at Paris and in London, as an eventuality, the Marshal received then, not the instructions they could not be given at such a distance, but the following advice.

"To obtain exact information of the strength of the Russian force in the Crimea. If not too considerable, to land at a spot which might serve as a basis for operations." * * * The article in the Moniteur, of which the above is an extract, is chiefly interesting as being supposed to represent the opinions and views of the Emperor Napoleon, who, as is well known, constantly offered suggestions and advice in the strategic movements during the war, and whose opinions naturally had great weight with the French Commanders. It will be necessary to make a further quotation shortly.

The move of the English army to Varna immediately displayed its unfitness for operations in the field. The Commissariat was in difficulties at once. Turkey is not a country prepared for large and sudden demands on its resources. The mere feeding the army was consequently no easy matter. And when some of the divisions moved a few miles inland, the question of transport gave rise to so much difficulty, that an establishment of men-of-war's boats was formed on the Lake of Devna to assist in carrying food, &c. As for advancing to the Danube (even if it had been advisable), it was out of the question. The army would have starved. In fact the want of transport became a serious evil. I have already said that nothing of the kind had been brought from England; the old waggon train of the Duke of Wellington had long fallen a victim to the school of financial reformers, and the economy of successive governments. To resuscitate it on the breaking out of hostilities in time to be of service was impossible.

As much of the transport of the army, during the war in Spain, had been carried on by means of the hired muleteers of the country, the English Government, apparently taking this as a precedent, seem to have considered that the resources of Turkey would in like manner have been sufficient for the purpose; and, therefore, beyond giving Mr Filder (with whom, as head of the commissariat, rested the responsibility of this branch) ample means to purchase or procure what was required, they took no other active or efficient steps to provide for moving the supplies of the army. But Turkey, a poor and a miserably provided country for all purposes of even ordinary traffic, possessed no resources adequate to meet the sudden demands of two large armies. Consequently, although Omar Pasha lent his assistance, and although English officers were sent in various directions to purchase, the result only proved to be a miserable collection of carts, drawn by oxen or buffaloes, whose drivers either from fear or laziness deserted if they could; and a herd of ponies with pack saddles of a most inferior and unserviceable kind.

But even if the resources of the country had been ample, it is an error to suppose that the mere collection of drivers and animals constitutes an effective transport corps, or that such can be considered otherwise than as auxiliaries. Without discipline or organization, disorder soon prevails, the animals fall out of condition, and the department becomes weakened. A transport corps requires time and study in its way, fully as much as the other branches of an army, and the want of it was one of the great difficulties of the English in the march in the Crimea, and one of the causes of their extreme suffering during the first winter before Sebastopol.

CHAPTER III.

THE raising of the siege of Silistria, and retreat of the Russians towards the end of June, at once gave evidence that their aggressive powers in that direction had been overrated, and set the allied armies at liberty for other operations. The English Government had, from the first, kept in view an expedition to the Crimea, and in July instructions were sent to Lord Raglan accordingly.

The report of the Committee of the House of Commons on the " State of the army before Sebastopol " relates the circumstances very clearly. It says :—

" The responsibility of the expedition to the Crimea rests upon the Home Government. The Duke of Newcastle in his dispatch addressed to Lord Raglan, on the 10th of April, 1854, directs careful but secret inquiry to be made into the present amount and condition of the Russian force in the Crimea, and the strength of the fortress of Sebastopol. And his Grace further observes that, before the siege of a fortress so strong can be attempted, it is neces-

sary that information which can be relied on shall be
obtained upon many points on which little or nothing
is at present known.

" A second despatch, dated the 29th June, directs
that, the safety of Constantinople having been secured,
whatever might be the movement of the Russian
forces, no campaign in the Principalities should be
undertaken, but that measures should at once be con-
certed for the siege of Sebastopol. There is, it is
added, no prospect of a safe and honourable peace
until the fortress is reduced, and the fleet taken or
destroyed. The despatch leaves to Lord Raglan a
discretion only in case of some insuperable impediment, such as a want of ample preparation by either
army, or of the possession by Russia of a force in the
Crimea greatly out-numbering that which can be
brought against it.

" The Cabinet appear to have been confident of
success. Lord Aberdeen states it to have been their
impression that Sebastopol would fall almost immediately by a *coup-de-main*. The Duke of Newcastle
says that he expected the army, after capturing Sebastopol, would winter there, or else, after destroying
the fortress, would return to winter on the shores of
the Bosphorus. Sir James Graham has the strong-
est opinion that the order for the expedition was
given at the right time, and was executed at the
right time.   *   *   *

" Your committee have inquired what information
the Government had obtained, which induced them to

order this expedition. In regard to this matter, it may be observed that the Duke of Newcastle had, in his despatch of the 10th April, estimated the Russian forces in the Crimea at 30,000 men, and he believes that when the expedition was ordered, no more re-liable accounts had been received. Sir James Graham says, however, that at a later period, namely, the last week in July, he had obtained from a Crimean authority a complete account of the Crimea, its local-ities, its harbours, its roads, its productions, and supply of water ; and, what was most important of all, a statement of the force, which was estimated by his informant at 70,000 men, 8000 of which were cavalry, 40,000 constituted the garrison of Sebas-topol, and the remaining 30,000 were dispersed through the Crimea. Vice Admiral Dundas had, on the 10th May, 1854, written to Lord Raglan a letter, in which, relying on information which he had obtained, he estimated the Russian forces in the Crimea at 120,000 men. The embassies at St. Petersburg and Constantinople were unable to furnish any information upon these important subjects."

On the receipt of his despatches, Lord Raglan, not-withstanding his own opinions were against the expe-dition, decided that it was his duty to carry out the orders of his Government. In his answer dated 19th July, he says,—" The descent on the Crimea is decided upon, more in deference to the views of the British Government, than to any information in the possession of the naval and military authorities, either as to the

extent of the enemy's forces, or to their state of preparation." St. Arnaud's instructions, as has been
shown, were to the same purpose as Lord Raglan's,
but with a wider discretion.

After the expedition had been decided upon, and
in the interval which elapsed before it could be
carried into execution, it is well known that great
differences of opinion existed among the generals and
admirals of both nations, as to its expediency. Various
circumstances caused delay, and certainly added very
.much to the responsibility which already attached
itself to so great an undertaking. The late season of
the year,—the uncertainty which still prevailed as to
the actual force of Russians in the Crimea, and of the
condition of the land defences of Sebastopol, added
to the physical weakness of the allied armies, and the
reduction of their numbers from cholera and fever,—
were all matters of grave consideration. But Lord
Raglan did not consider these circumstances sufficient
to induce him to alter his previous decision, and was
perfectly unmoved by the gloomy views entertained
by some, as to the probably disastrous fate of the
expedition.

During the month of August, active preparations
were made. The English transports assembled at
Varna and Balchik; rafts and paddle-box boats were
fitted for landing horses and artillery. Regiments
were employed in making gabions, fascines, &c. Still
many doubted the reality of the expedition; until on
the 25th of August Marshal St. Arnaud issued a

proclamation to the French army, in which he informed them that Providence had called them to the Crimea, a country healthy as France ; and finally, that ere long the three united flags should float over the ramparts of Sebastopol !   Lord Raglan also issued his instructions, commencing as follows : " The invasion of the Crimea having been determined on, the troops will embark in such ships as shall be provided for their conveyance."

Towards the end of August, the armies commenced embarking.

The general idea of the Governments of England and France in deciding upon the invasion of the Crimea, and reduction of Sebastopol, appears to have been, that its accomplishment could be achieved in one campaign, that is, before the arrival of winter. Supposing the landing to be successful, it seems to have been calculated, that after an action with the enemy in the open country Sebastopol might be invested, and, not being regularly fortified on the land front, would probably afford no lengthened resistance.

The great sickness of the armies, the late arrival of the French siege train, and the necessity of preparing rafts and boats, were causes of delay in the departure of the expedition.   The time and means afforded were thus barely sufficient if all went well.   But the English Government does not appear to have taken into consideration the alternative of non-success, or to have calculated the consequences which must ensue (with both armies compromised to the attempt) if winter should arrive and find them still with open trenches before the city.

The report of the Committee of the House of Commons on the subject is as follows :—

" Your committee report that the suffering of the army resulted mainly from the circumstances under which the expedition to the Crimea was undertaken and executed. The administration which ordered that expedition had no adequate information as to the amount of the forces in the Crimea. They were not acquainted with the strength of the fortresses to be attacked, or with the resources of the country to be invaded. They hoped and expected the expedition to be immediately successful, and, as they did not foresee the probability of a protracted struggle, they made no provision for a winter campaign."

Varna, with the ordinary helplessness of an oriental town, offered no facilities, such as wharfs, &c., for even ordinary traffic, much less for the sudden embarkation of two large armies with all their vast material. Its defects had been partially remedied by the construction of temporary wharfs and stages on the shores of the Bay. From these the English infantry were conveyed to their respective ships in the boats of the fleet, and in small steamers of light draft; the cavalry and artillery horses, the guns, waggons, &c., on rafts, formed of two paddle-box or other boats, lashed together, with a stage fixed on the top of them. So excellent were the arrangements and details of the naval authorities in this important matter, that the whole of the army was embarked in the course of a few days, in 29 large steamers, and 56 sailing ships; and the transports as they successively loaded, proceeded at once to Balchik Bay, the general rendezvous.

The detail of the numbers embarked is about as follows.

Detail.	Men.	Horses.	Guns.	Remarks.
* 5 Divisions of Infantry	25,200	350†	....	† The General and Regimental Staff Horses of the whole army.
1 Division of Cavalry	1200	1200		
Field Artillery { 2 Troops ...... { 8 Batteries ...	2000	1800	60	6 Prs.————— 4 12 Pr. Howrs.——— 2 9 Prs.————— 36 24 Pr. Howrs.—— 18 ————— 60
Siege Artillery	800	....	60†	† Heavy Guns with 500 rounds per gun. † Guns of position with 100 rounds per gun.
Sappers	400		60†	
For Reserve Infantry Ammn.	....	850†	....	† With Turkish Drivers.
	29,600	4200	180†	

* One division with its artillery was embarked in the Bosphorus.

A large amount of field artillery and infantry reserve ammunition, engineer and siege train stores, &c., were also embarked.†

During the voyage to the Crimea the fleet of transports conveying the English army sailed in six parallel lines, each line containing a division. The infantry were chiefly on board the steamers, each of which took in tow two sailing ships, full of artillery, ammunition, and stores.

The embarkation of the French army took place simultaneously with our own, but, owing to want of means of transport, their arrangements were of a totally different character. Their infantry was embarked on board the line-of-battle ships and steamers of their squadron, none of the former having less than 700 on board; and many of their ships embarked nearly 2000 men in addition to their crews. The Turkish fleet was encumbered in the same way with about 6000 of their own troops; so that, in fact, the English fleet alone was in a condition to meet the enemy in case they had been bold enough to take the sea: and on the English Admiral therefore devolved in great measure the responsibility of guarding the enormous convoy.

The numbers of the French embarked were nearly as follows. 4 divisions of infantry,=24,000 men; with 68 field and 65 siege guns, and 2900 horses. Their total of all ranks, including sappers, intendance, &c., was about 30,000.

† The department of the Commissariat is not included in the above.

CHAPTER IV.

In proceeding to the Crimea, the point of disembarkation became the first and most important subject for decision. The French views are explained in the following quotation from the Moniteur:*—

" Theodosia (Kaffa) appeared the most eligible spot; although that point of the coast has the disadvantage of being distant 40 leagues from Sebastopol, it nevertheless offers great advantages. First, its bay is vast and safe. It could hold all the vessels of the squadron, and the vessels with provisions for the troops. Secondly, once established on that point it might be made a real basis for operations.

" In thus occupying the eastern point of the Crimea, all the reinforcements coming by the Sea of Azoff and the Caucasus would be cut off; a gradual advance could be made towards the centre of the country, taking advantage of all its resources. Simpheropol, the strategic centre of the peninsula, would

* It must be borne in mind that it was written months after the landing in the Crimea.

be occupied. An advance would thus be made upon Sebastopol, and probably a great battle fought on that road. If lost, a retreat in good order on Kaffa, and nothing is compromised; if gained, to besiege Sebastopol, to invest it completely, and its surrender would follow as a matter of course, in a short interval.

"Unhappily these counsels were not followed. Be it, that the Commanders-in-Chief had not sufficient troops to take so long a journey in the Crimea; be it, that they expected a more speedy, result by a bold and sudden *coup-de-main*, they resolved, as is known, to land at a few leagues only from Sebastopol."

A pamphlet published lately gives a curious account of a discussion that took place on this subject, during the voyage to the Crimea, and shows plainly that even to the last the French Marshal was undecided in his plans. As follows :—

"At this period a remarkable incident occurred, which has been glanced at, and but imperfectly described. A signal was made from the French flagship, to the effect that Marshal St. Arnaud was desirous of conferring with Admiral Dundas and Lord Raglan, and being too unwell to pass to them, they were requested to repair to the Ville-de-Paris, where he was, having something of importance to communicate. Lord Raglan was on board the steamer Caradoc, alongside the Britannia, from which latter the English Admiral went to his lordship and communicated the message, and it was arranged that they should proceed in the Caradoc to the Ville-de-Paris. On arriving under that ship it was agreed that Admiral Dundas should go on board, Lord Raglan being unable to do so, having lost an arm. Accordingly the Admiral visited the Marshal, who was found seated in the cabin, suffering extreme pain, and unable to converse. He pointed to a paper lying on the table, which the Admiral read ; it had no signature or any passage to show from whom it proceeded. Marshal St Arnaud was unable to speak and therefore could not explain or rectify the omission. The paper urged that it would be too hazardous to attempt the landing at the Katcha river (which had heretofore been the point contemplated for disembarkation) ; that the English press had published, and in Parliament it had been made known to the enemy, that the allies had fixed upon that point as the place of debarkation, to which, of course, the Russian force would have been drawn to oppose the landing ; that the season of the year was too advanced for a siege of Sebastopol, the garrison of which was known to be stronger than had been anticipated ; that the enemy was powerful in the arm of cavalry, in which the allies were almost wholly deficient, and this for operations in a country adapted for the movement of that nature of force. From these considerations it was necessary to reconsider the measures to be adopted.

" Admiral Dundas hereupon descended to the Caradoc, accompanied by the French Generals.

The paper was read to Lord Raglan, whose first observation was the very natural question, from whom
that document proceeded; a question which was not
answered. A long and anxious debate took place,
and it was urged that Theodosia (Kaffa) would be the
preferable point of the Crimea at which to land.
This place is on the eastern coast of the peninsula,
at 70 miles from Sebastopol, and at 20 miles from
Kertch.

" At length the discussion was terminated by Lord
Raglan declaring that he would not now consent to
alter a decision which had been come to after much
deliberation in the last council at Varna. The only
result of this scene was, that the coast from Eupatoria
to Sebastopol should be reconnoitred, and the point of
disembarkation between those places finally determined. A copy of the paper alluded to was demanded,
but was not subsequently afforded."

With respect to the project of landing at Kaffa
(Theodosia); in the first place it was distant from
Sebastopol, and the armies were physically unfit for
long marches; they were also, numerically, too weak to
undertake a campaign in the heart of the Crimea, distant from their supplies, and from the fleet; besides
which, neither army had sufficient means of land
transport. In addition to all these powerful reasons,
a difficulty would have arisen from the deficiency of
water in this part of the country,—the Salghir being
the only river of any size; so that had the allied
armies landed at Kaffa, the probabilities are, that

Showing the English Regiments of the Light, First

with the number of

LIGHT DIVISION.

Sir George Brown.

Rifle Battn.

Sir George Buller. | | Sir William Codrington.

77th Regt.	88th Regt.	19th Regt.	23rd Regt.	33rd Regt.	7th Reg
18	23	226	210	239	229

FIRST DIVISION.

H. R. H. Duke of Cambridge.

Sir C. Campbell. | | | General Bentinck.
(Highland Brigade. | | | (Guards Brigade.)

79th Regt.	93rd Regt.	42nd Regt.	Coldstreams.	Scots Fuslrs.	G
9	52	37	80	181	

The numbers in the square

Each Regiment

nd Divisions, as they stood at the Battle of Alma,
in each Regiment.

SECOND DIVISION.

Sir de Lacy Evans.

	Sir J. Pennefather.			General Adams.		
. Regt.	55th Regt.	30th Regt.	47th Regt.	49th Regt.	41st Regt.
93	115	79	69		

casualties in each Regiment.

800 strong.

they would either have advanced to disaster, or, finding themselves unequal to the attempt, have remained inactive at the place of disembarkation.

The fact is, that the enterprise was a bold and dangerous one; undertaken at a late season of the year with an inadequate force; and its best chance of success rested in ignoring ordinary rules of war, and in landing near Sebastopol, and taking it, if possible, before succour could arrive. The attempt failed in the first instance, and only succeeded in the end, at great cost of time, money, and human life.

The coast of the Crimea from Kaffa to Kameisch being mountainous, afforded no points for disembarkation on that side, except at Balaclava, which, however, was too small a port for such an extensive operation. The allies consequently had but little option in this respect, and resolved upon landing to the north of Sebastopol, where the country was flat and open, the beach available in many places, and through which flowed several small rivers.

In consequence of the discussion already spoken of, this part of the coast was again carefully examined at the last moment by Lord Raglan himself. The beach at the mouth of the river Katcha (which had previously been fixed upon) was found to be too limited in extent; and being also commanded by heights on both sides, at short artillery range, the enemy, who were in force in the neighbourhood, might have rendered the disembarkation difficult, if not impossible.

Some miles to the north was a long flat beach, where the operation could be flanked and protected by guns from the ships, and this point was accordingly decided upon. Its chief disadvantage proved to be the scarcity of fresh water.

CHAPTER V.

THE English transports anchored in the Bay of
Eupatoria on the afternoon of the 13th; the place
itself surrendering to a flag of truce. The landing at
Old Fort commenced early on the morning of the 14th
September. Owing to the fleet having weighed
anchor during the previous night, the transports had
not, in the darkness, been able to preserve the " order
of sailing " as correctly as they had hitherto done
during the voyage, so that on arriving off the shore
some confusion arose, which was rather increased by
the French exceeding their allotted limits of anchoring. Admiral Dundas also, apprehending an attack
from the Russian fleet, kept some of the English
men-of-war a considerable distance out to sea, so that
their boats detailed for the purpose of landing the
troops were not immediately available. Some delay
was thus caused at the commencement on the part of
the English, which, however, was only temporary, the
whole of the infantry of the army, and 20 guns
horsed, with ammunition, &c., being on shore before

3 *

evening. The arrangements of the French were admirable, and from their account it appears that three of their divisions, with a numerous artillery, were also landed the first day. Their fourth division, in order to divide the attention of the enemy, feigned a disembarkation at the Katcha.

It has always appeared rather inexplicable why Prince Menschikoff should have allowed so difficult an operation, on the part of the allies, and one which extended over five days, to be completed without any attempt on his part either to oppose or delay it. Even partial or false attacks at night would have been very harassing. The probabilities are, that he was occupied in concentrating his troops, and that he relied implicitly for victory on the strong position he took up on the heights beyond the Alma. During the four days succeeding, the allies were constantly and indefatigably engaged in landing the remainder of their troops, field artillery, horses, waggons, ammunition, and stores. Their operations were retarded for two days by a heavy surf on the beach.

The Baron de Bazancourt, who, in his history of the war, takes frequent occasion to criticize the conduct of the English, and to contrast their operations unfavourably as compared with those of his own countrymen, states, that on this occasion the latter were delayed for two days after their arrangements were complete, owing to the tardiness of the English, and he quotes a private letter from Marshal St Arnaud to that effect. But the circumstances of the two armies were not parallel. The French only landed four horses per gun, and a very small amount of artillery and infantry reserve ammunition. They had no cavalry. The English on the contrary had a force of 1200 cavalry ; they had to put on shore 850 pack-horses for the conveyance of an infantry reserve of ammunition. Their guns had eight horses each, and their batteries were complete in all their waggons, ammunition, and stores. The French, with their right resting on the sea, with their left protected by the English, having thus both flanks and rear guarded, and having a ready and constant access to the beach, might venture to advance, thus lightly equipped and with small reserves.* Not so with those on the outward flank, whose front flank and rear were all liable to attack, and who, being miles distant from the sea, could not at any moment replenish their supplies, and therefore could not venture on such provisional arrangements. The extra number of horses, waggons, ammunition, and stores thus required, will sufficiently explain the alleged tardiness, all these requiring time, and being more difficult of disembarkation than troops, as is evident from the fact, that the great bulk of the infantry of both armies were landed during the first few hours. The troops suffered severely from the scarcity of water, also from cholera and fever, during these first few days.

* In his despatch of the battle of Alma, St. Arnaud confesses that the ammunition of his artillery was exhausted ; which is a proof how little he had landed, for it was not an action in which any large proportion was expended.

Had the allies been in overpowering strength, and had they possessed means of rapid movement, it is probable their advance would have been at once towards the centre of the Crimea; as a victory gained at that point would have given them the command of the country, and have thus insured the fall of Sebastopol. But the season was late; neither army was provided with sufficient land transport : they had no safe base of operations to fall back upon in case of need; all these circumstances deprived them of the power of choice, and controlled the direction of their march along the sea-shore; by which means they preserved their communication with the fleets, from which latter they received both supplies and support.

Owing to the want of transport, the officers and men of the English army were obliged to carry for themselves three days' provisions ; and they also slept at night without cover, from the impossibility of carrying the tents. The French were better off in this latter point, having small portable tentes-abris, which although affording incomplete shelter, were excellent as a temporary measure.*

The order of march of the divisions is shown in the accompanying diagram.

* Lord Raglan in his despatch after Alma, gives the reason why his troops were exposed to these unusual hardships. He says,—" My anxiety to bring into the country every cavalry and infantry soldier who was available, prevented me from embarking their baggage animals, and these officers have with them at this moment nothing but what they can carry, and they, equally with the men, are without tents or covering of any kind."

On the morning of the 19th of September the allied armies advanced on Sebastopol. The troops were in excellent spirits at the prospect of immediate action. The country was open and undulating; the distant smoke of burning villages, and the occasional appearance of a few Cossacks hovering in the front and on the left flank, were the only evidences that the march was being made in an enemy's country. The Russian cavalry on this, as on most occasions during the war, showed considerable wariness, and a want of that daring disposition which their former reputation had led one to expect.

The arrival at the small fresh stream of the Bulganac was most welcome to the men and horses of both armies, who for days had suffered from a scanty supply of indifferent water. Beyond it the ground rose slightly, and late in the afternoon the enemy's horsemen showed in considerable force. Lord Raglan therefore advanced with the English light cavalry (about 600 sabres) under the Earl of Cardigan, and, throwing out skirmishers, followed the enemy for some distance as they slowly withdrew across the plain. The Russians at length brought into action a battery of eight guns, which fired the first shots of the campaign, but it was speedily met by two troops of horse artillery, and the enemy then fell back, covered by a cloud of skirmishers. Lord Raglan, anxious to avoid any further collision at so late an hour, declined to follow them, and the allied forces then took up their positions and bivouacked for the night.

On that evening, when the staff officers attended for orders, General Airey, the Quarter-Master-General, stated that the Russian army, consisting of about 40 battalions, with a powerful artillery, was close at hand, posted on the heights beyond the Alma, and that a general action was imminent on the morrow.

CHAPTER VI.

BATTLE OF THE ALMA.

" Though till now ungraced in story, scant although thy waters be,
   Alma, roll those waters proudly ; roll them proudly to the sea."

ON the morning of the 20th of September, 1854,
the position taken up by the allied troops was as follows : — Commencing from the beach, the French
columns were clustered along the ridge of gentle hills
extending inland.   Their piquets were some hundred
yards in advance, and, although they had only been
one night on the ground, had already covered themselves with slight earthworks.   Where the French
columns ended (Prince Napoleon's division being the
last), the English commenced, and prolonged the line.
The ground in front of the position sloped gently
away to the Alma, about three miles distant, with
villages, orchards, and gardens spread out along its
banks.

On the other side of the river the ground at once
rose suddenly and precipitously to the height of three
or four hundred feet, with table land at the top.   This
range of heights, which, particularly near the sea, was

so steep as to be almost inaccessible, continued for about two miles along the south bank, and then broke away from the river (making a deep curve round an amphitheatre as it were, about a mile wide), and then returned to the stream again, but with gentler slopes and features of a much less abrupt character.

It was upon this latter part that Prince Menschi-koff had posted the right of his army (see plan), and as the road to Sebastopol crossed the river by a wooden bridge just below, and as this point was, in fact, the key of the position, and most liable to attack, great preparations had been made for its defence. About half way down the slope, a large earthen bat-tery had been made, partially enfilading the front, in which were twelve heavy guns of position (A), and higher up and in its right rear, was another of four guns (B), sweeping the ground in that direction. Dense columns of infantry were massed on the slopes, with large reserves on the heights above. A lower ridge of hills ran across the amphitheatre, and at vari-ous points batteries of field artillery were posted, commanding the passage of the river and its ap-proaches. In front of this part of the position, and on our side of the river, was the village of Bourliuk.

Upon the long range of heights first spoken of, and in front of the French, the enemy had established their left, with reserves also in rear of their left centre. This part of the position was of such great natural strength, and more especially towards the sea the ac-clivities were so abrupt, that, considering themselves safe from attack, they had not extended their left far in this direction, so that when General Bosquet gained the heights overlooking the village of Alma-tamak, he only encountered at first a few Cossacks. The enemy had even neglected to scarp or guard the few narrow paths which led up the slopes.

The river, which with numerous windings flowed along the whole front, was fordable at most points, but its banks were steep, and there / were only occasional places at which artillery could readily be got across. A numerous body of Russian riflemen on our side of the river found excellent cover among the villages, gardens, and vineyards spread along its banks.

Such is an outline of the manner in which Prince Menschikoff had skilfully disposed of an army numbering about 40,000 men, with 80 field and other guns of large calibre. Fearing for his right, as affording fewer natural obstacles, it was there he had concentrated his chief strength to command the road ; and beyond this flank again a numerous cavalry was held in readiness for such contingencies as the battle might create. The disposition of the Russian forces is indicated on the map.

As to the plan of attack of the allies, De Bazancourt states that the design originated by Marshal St. Arnaud was, that the English should turn the enemy's right, at the same time that General Bosquet's division, reinforced by the Turks, should climb the steep heights at the river's mouth, and turn their left. The

1st and 3rd French divisions (with the 4th in reserve) then to attack the centre. But the troops in this last attack were not to advance until an hour after the others.

Such a plan is at once open to great objections. The forces would have been divided into three distinct parts, besides which, it is at all times dangerous to attempt to turn simultaneously both flanks of an enemy, unless the attacking force is very superior in numbers (which in this instance was not the case); but more particularly would it have been so with an enemy posted and intrenched on strong ground of their own choosing, and with a river in their front.

Lord Raglan in his despatch does not allude to these propositions, but states,—" It was arranged that Marshal St. Arnaud should assail the enemy's left, by crossing the river at its junction with the sea and immediately above it; and that the remainder of the French divisions should move up the heights in their front, whilst the English army should attack the right and centre of the enemy's position." St. Arnaud in writing to the Minister-at-War says,—" It had been arranged with Lord Raglan that his troops should perform a movement to their left turning the enemy's flank analogous to that which General Bosquet effected on the right; but, incessantly threatened by cavalry, and outflanked by the Russians on the heights, the English army was obliged to relinquish this part of the programme."

The reasons given by St. Arnaud for its relinquishment at once explain under what totally different circumstances any flank attack would have been made by the English, as compared with a similar movement on the part of General Bosquet. The latter had comparatively no enemy at all in his front, and received little opposition until he had gained the heights. His advance was flanked and supported by the steamers of the fleet, and if he had failed in maintaining himself, his retreat to the beach would have been protected in the same way; whereas the English had the main body of the Russian army directly in their front, and a powerful cavalry on the flank, held aloof, and ready to act against them. If they had attempted a turning movement and had failed, they would have been separated from their allies and from the fleet, on which latter they entirely depended for supplies.

Lord Raglan, so far from attempting any movement of the kind, before going down to the battle refused his assent to it; and it was decided that the English attack should commence when the French troops had gained the crest of the hills in their own front. Consequently, on arriving in front of Bourliuk, Lord Raglan deployed his first line, and having brought his artillery into action in the intervals of brigades, held his men back and made them lie down, waiting to advance until the French had partially completed their forward movement and had shaken the enemy's left. He then gave the word, and the English went straight up the hill. Thus the battle resolved itself into an *échelon* attack from the right of the allied

armies; Bosquet beginning; the other French divisions following; and the English completing the
movement. When it is considered that the base of
our operations was the sea-shore, and that our safety
depended on a free communication with the fleets, it
will probably be admitted that Lord Raglan showed
good judgment in not attempting anything so
dangerous as an inland flank movement; and therefore when De Bazancourt calls the direct advance of
the English an " heroic error," he pronounces an unjust
libel on one of the most brilliant feats ever performed
by an army.

It has been suggested that the allies, by a flank
march inland, might have drawn the enemy from their
position, and thus have avoided fighting them on their
own ground; but such a movement, involving the
abandonment of the sea-board, would (without
materially altering the relative advantages of the
enemy) have been most hazardous, and would have
risked the fortunes of the allies altogether on the issue
of a single battle. As it was, the risk was sufficiently
great.

It had been intended that the general advance of
the allies should have taken place at the early hour;
but some considerable delay was caused owing to the
numerous cases of cholera and sickness in the English
army during the previous night. Our position being
on the outward and unprotected flank, the whole of
these had to be collected and conveyed along the rear
of both armies to the beach for embarkation; and the

limited means of transport at our command (being a few country arabas drawn by oxen) added to the difficulty. The French being close to the sea had naturally great advantages in this respect. De Bazancourt is of opinion that this delay prevented the enemy from being taken by surprise, and that they were able to divine our plans, and alter their dispositions accordingly ; but as their ground was already taken up, their position intrenched, and as they were fully aware of the coming attack, the facts would scarcely seem to warrant his conclusion.

During the morning, Marshal St. Arnaud rode along the front of the two armies to meet Lord Raglan and make final arrangements for the battle. In personal appearance the French Marshal was pale, thin, bent, and emaciated, but he seemed in good spirits, and pleased when the English cheered him heartily as he passed. There was certainly something touching and chivalrous in the feeling which induced him, even in his last hours, when suffering from a mortal disease, and daily growing more feeble, to remain still at the head of his army and lead it in the field.

At about eleven a.m. the allied armies advanced, the whole front covered by a chain of light infantry. On the extreme right, and about 1500 yards in advance of the line, was the division of General Bosquet ; next on his left was that of General Canrobert ; then the Prince Napoleon's, with General Forey's in his rear in reserve. The English then took up the alignment, commencing

with the 2nd division (Sir de L. Evans), then
the light division (Sir G. Brown), and in rear of
these the 3rd and 1st divisions respectively, the
whole in column — Sir G. Cathcart with the 4th
division being in reserve, and on the outward flank—
the English cavalry, under the Earl of Lucan, considerably farther to the left, also protecting the
exposed flank and rear.

As the division of Bosquet approached the
river, his two brigades separated; one (accompanied by the Turks) keeping close to the shore,
crossed the river by the bar, at its very mouth;
but the heights on the south side were so steep
that the troops could then only proceed by files
up a foot-path, impracticable for artillery; consequently this brigade, though unopposed (its front
having been cleared by shells from the steamers),
could not regain its formation on the crest, until
a considerable time after the other had been engaged.

The other brigade inclining to its left passed
by the village of Alma-tamak, and, receiving trifling
opposition, in a few minutes reached the summit.
Two batteries of artillery were got up with difficulty, and at once opened fire to their left *en
potence* along the heights. It was about noon.

The enemy, taken by surprise at an attack on
their left, where they had least expected it, and
where they had considered the ground impracticable, detached at once several batteries and other

troops from their centre to meet it, and Bosquet's artillery became heavily engaged, but not at very close range.   St. Arnaud, taking advantage of the success of this manœuvre, and in order to prevent General Bosquet from being overpowered, on the firing of the first gun at once ordered the columns of General Canrobert and Prince Napoleon to attack in their front.   In advancing they were warmly received at the river by the Russian skirmishers, and by their infantry on the slopes.   The French artillery was brought into action, the batteries of Prince Napoleon being placed on the right of the village of Bourliuk (see plan).   The French columns soon forced the passage of the river, and began to swarm up the heights, the enemy gradually retiring before them, but disputing every inch of ground.   It was about two p.m. when the French gained the crest, and Canrobert then found himself face to face with the left centre of the Russian army, consisting of powerful columns, concentrated near an unfinished telegraph tower.   His own artillery had been obliged to make a détour to gain the heights, and had not joined him : that of the enemy, hitherto engaged with Bosquet, now turned and concentrated their fire upon his columns.   The Prince Napoleon, on his left, also met with equal opposition.   St. Arnaud then ordered forward General Forey's two brigades of the reserve.   Arriving with their artillery, they gave timely support to Generals Can·

4

robert and the Prince Napoleon ; at the same time
Bosquet continued to advance along the heights
and threatened the Russian left, which enabled
Canrobert to order an attack to the front, and
the enemy were then driven back, retreating with
heavy loss.

Thus far the battle in this direction was gained; the French having accomplished a most difficult and gallant advance, for which their activity
and dashing qualities were well suited. But a
sterner and far more terrible struggle had commenced upon the left.

The two leading English divisions (the light
and second) which had advanced across the plain
in alignment with the French columns, on coming within long range of the enemy's guns, deployed into line (two deep), and whilst waiting for
the further development of the French attack
were ordered to lie down, so as to present as
small a mark as possible. The Russian batteries
opened, and it was evident that many of their
guns were of large calibre ; fortunately their fire
was rather plunging, and therefore not very effective against a thin line. The Russian riflemen,
concealed in the village and its enclosures, also
opened fire, and the village itself suddenly burst
into flames and obscured by its smoke the position
of the enemy, especially in front of the 2nd division.

During this time the English batteries of the
first line were in action ; but the enemy's guns

were more numerous, and many of them of heavier calibre; they were placed in commanding positions, and covered by intrenchments, or by undulations of the ground; consequently the English batteries, exposed on an open plain and firing at long range, fought at a disadvantage.

The two supporting divisions, a few hundred yards in rear of the leading ones, also shortly deployed.

Meanwhile the French columns, as already described, had crossed the river in their own front, and were hotly engaged, driving the Russian skirmishers up the steep acclivities on the other side. It appears that Sir de Lacy Evans received a message from the French Marshal, to the effect that his troops, having gained the heights, were threatened by large bodies of the Russians, and that it would be advisable to divert the attention of the enemy by pressing them in our front. It was probably about the same time that Lord Raglan received a similar communication. The moment of action had arrived.

About half an hour had elapsed from the time that the two English divisions had deployed until they received their final order to advance. Lord Raglan having given the order passed with his staff by the right of the burning village, and came suddenly down upon a ford of the river. The enemy's riflemen, concealed behind the banks and walls on the other side, and whose attention

4 *

was naturally turned to the points which offered
the greatest facilities for crossing, on the appearance
of so large a body of horsemen poured in a
very sharp fire.   Lord Raglan, however, pushed
across, and galloped forward, passing on his right
some French troops in the vineyards, and soon
reached commanding ground, being, in fact, one
of the lower spurs of the heights, up which the
troops of Napoleon's division were climbing. This
point was on the extreme left of the French attack,
and just at the angle where the range of heights
ceased to follow the course of the stream.

In advance of, and separated for the moment from,
his army, and on the flank of that part of the position
which his own troops were about to storm, Lord
Raglan, who could now plainly distinguish the position
of the Russian columns and batteries, at once perceived the important advantage he should gain, could
an artillery fire be opened from the spot where he
stood.   He despatched accordingly an urgent message
for some guns.   A battery of the 2nd division was
close to the ford but had not crossed it.   Two of its
guns were speedily brought up to the desired point,
and the remainder of the battery soon followed.   Its
fire directed against the Russian columns and batteries on the opposite slopes, and who were now very
heavily engaged with the general advance of the light
and second divisions, had a powerful effect not only
materially, but also morally, as showing the enemy
that whilst their front was being stormed, their flank

was already turned. The battery moved subsequently up the heights, and harassed the Russian columns in their retreat.

In the mean time the two leading divisions advanced steadily across the plain towards the enemy, with the rifles and some skirmishers of the 2nd division in advance, General Codrington's brigade leading straight for the Russian intrenched battery. The two brigades of the 2nd division coming down upon the village, and unable to force their way through the burning ruins, separated, that of General Pennefather (supported by one regiment* of General Adams) inclining to its left, and thus keeping up its connection with the light division. General Adams, with his two remaining regiments, passed by the right of the village, crossed the river with the guns already named, and, after considerable opposition and delay from the difficulties in getting over, passed up the heights on the French left, where the brigade deployed and was again joined by the 47th regiment. It then advanced along the plateau, between the Sebastopol road and the telegraph tower, and was thus in a position, at the close, to have inflicted additional loss on the broken Russian columns, had the French supported it in a forward movement.

The brigade of General Pennefather (whose regiments from want of space were crowded and had never, therefore, been perfectly deployed) moved by the left of the village close to the Sebastopol road,

* 47th regiment.

and on approaching the bridge by which it crosses the Alma, found itself in the very centre of the enemy's position, and at the focus towards which their heaviest fire, both of artillery and musketry, was directed. Seeking a temporary shelter in the gardens and enclosures on either side, the regiments continued heavily engaged for a considerable time, and suffered severe loss, the enemy strenuously resisting every attempt made to force the position. Three batteries of the light, first, and second divisions respectively, which in their advance had converged towards this point for the purpose of crossing, now also came into action, and being at a more convenient range, gave material support to the infantry, as they gradually forced the passage. The batteries, subsequently, on the other side also rendered effective service in maintaining the ground.

Whilst the battle thus raged in its centre, and whilst Pennefather's brigade, in thus insisting at this point, greatly occupied the enemy and thereby gave effectual support to the advance of the light division, it becomes necessary now to turn to the latter. The regiments composing it moved steadily across the plain in a long thin line. Their ranks, however, became broken to a certain extent, owing to the gardens, vineyards, and walls over which they had to pass as they approached the river, and still more so, by the inequalites and holes in its bed, as they crossed it. The companies of the rifle brigade in advance on the left were the first across, and were then in close vicinity to large bodies of the enemy. The somewhat straggling line of the light division found a momentary indifferent shelter behind the broken ground, as it rose on the opposite bank. It has been urged that advantage might have been taken of this circumstance to regain a more correct formation of the line, but to have checked the eagerness of the troops at such a moment, under a terrific fire of grape and musketry, and with the enemy close at hand, would have been insanity, and would probably have been fatal to success. Sir George Brown was far too good a soldier to entertain such an idea.

It was a moment of intense anxiety as the light division jumped from their cover, and with a rattling fire commenced the charge. The ground over which they now had to pass was of the nature of a steep smooth glacis. On the left it was more undulating, and the two regiments in that direction (77th and 88th) being thus more protected, and not being in the direct line of fire, suffered comparatively little ; and having to form square, on being threatened there by the enemy's cavalry, they took no very active part in the great stuggle. General Codrington's brigade,* however, with the 19th on their left, and the 95th on their right, were now in direct line and in full view of the great Russian battery.

Hitherto every advantage had been on the side of the enemy. The ground was of their own choosing ; their numerous artillery, which was partially in-

* 33rd and 23rd Regiments, and 7th Fusiliers.

trenched, swept all the approaches from commanding points. The English regiments had not only had to advance under a crushing fire, but whilst subject to it, to cross a river and numerous other obstacles. Much had already been done by them, but still more remained. The scale, however, began in some degree to turn in their favour. As the English line approached the Russian columns, its formation, straggling and irregular as it was, allowed its regiments at once to open a continuous line of fire. The enemy's columns could be seen opening out and endeavouring to extend their front, but it was too late; the light division was close upon them. Then the Russian columns began to shake; then men from the rear were seen to run; then whole columns would turn and fly, halting again, and facing about at short intervals; but with artillery smashing on their left flank, with Codrington's brigade supported by Pennefather's, still streaming upwards, and every moment pouring in their fire, nearer and nearer as they rushed up the slope, the enemy's troops could no longer maintain their ground, but fled disordered up the hill. The Russian batteries still, however, made a frightful havoc in the English ranks, and a wide street of dead and wounded lying on the ground the whole way from the river upwards showed the terrific nature of the fight.

Breathless, decimated, and much broken, but with victory crowning their efforts, the men of the centre regiments at length dashed over the intrenchment and into the great battery where they captured two guns.

That they did not find a greater number there, is a proof of the smartness and vigilance of the Russian gunners in thus working their guns, and being able to withdraw almost all of them at the last moment. But the trials of the light division were not yet at an end. The reserves of the enemy now moved down. The English regiments, their ranks in disarray and sorely thinned, were forced gradually to relinquish the ground they had gained, and doggedly fell back, followed by the Russian columns. It seemed for a moment as if victory still were doubtful, but succour was close at hand. The three regiments of Guards (having the Highland brigade on their left) were now steadily advancing up the hill, in magnificent order. There was a slight delay until the regiments of Codrington's brigade had passed through their ranks, during which time the struggle still wavered, and the casualties were very great; but when once their front was clear, the chance of the Russians was at an end, and their whole force retreated in confusion.

Lord Raglan, as soon as he had perceived the success of the flank fire from the French heights (previously described), galloped across the intervening valley and joined his troops as they ascended the hill. The several batteries of the different divisions, after crossing at the bridge moved rapidly to their front, and completed the victory by pouring in a heavy fire until the broken columns of the enemy were out of range.

The joy and excitement of the English troops were

intense as Lord Raglan rode along the line formed on
the heights they had just won.   It was a great victory,
not only in its immediate results, but in its general
effect on the Russian army.

A brilliant and in many respects an admirable
account is given of this battle by Mr. Russell, the
Times correspondent, in the latest edition of his
work on the Crimea; but it is to be observed, that
Mr. Russell, on this as on almost every occasion, appears to take equal pleasure with the Baron de
Bazancourt in imputing incapacity and blundering to
Lord Raglan, Sir George Brown, and most of the
superior officers of the English army; in fact, so
constantly does he portray them as ignorant of the
most ordinary knowledge of their profession, that his
remarks would almost appear to be dictated by personal feelings.   This is doubtless a great blemish, and
it is apparent throughout the work.   In his account
he especially criticizes the conduct of Sir George
Buller, who commanded the left brigade of the light
division, and censures that officer for not having taken
the 77th and 88th regiments, after crossing the river,
to the assistance of those who were so heavily engaged
at the great battery.   But he seems not to perceive,
that Sir George, being on the exposed flank, had a
distinct duty to perform in preventing its being turned
by the large Russian force (both of infantry and
cavalry) which was in that direction.   Had Sir George
Buller allowed those two regiments to move as suggested, the light division might have found itself cut

up in flank, at the moment it was overmatched in front. The proper reserve for Codrington's brigade was the one which came up to its support—that is, the guards; and even if General Buller did (as stated) throw his regiments into square before he was absolutely attacked, it is a proof at all events that his attention was turned to the particular point which it was his duty to watch.

Mr. Russell describes Lord Raglan at Alma as trotting in front of his army amid a shower of balls,— "with a kind nod for every one, and leaving his generals and men to fight it out as best they could; riding across the stream through the French riflemen, not knowing where he was going to, or where the enemy were, till fate led him to a little knoll, from which he saw some of the Russian guns on his flank, whereupon he sent an order to Turner's battery for guns, and seemed surprised that they could not be dragged across a stream, and up a hill which presented some difficulties to an unencumbered horseman—then cantering over to join the guards just ere they made their charge, and finding it all over while he was in a hollow of the ground." Now surely this is unworthy and untrue.

Mr. Russell speaking of the war also tells us that posterity "will pass a verdict in this cause which none of us can hope to influence or evade." Let us hope so. I have a sincere conviction, when the real facts of that great war are fully known, that the verdict of posterity will be far different to what the Times correspondent anticipates. Even now when so little true light has as yet been thrown upon the conduct of Lord Raglan, and upon the real causes of the English misfortunes in the campaign, the public are already beginning to perceive that the impressions they received at the time from irresponsible writers were very wide of the truth; and as to Mr. Russell's estimate of Lord Raglan's character and abilities as a general, I believe, at this moment, if the opinion of the allied admirals and generals (French, Sardinian, Turkish, and English) who were engaged in that war, were obtained, as to what man among them was more distinguished for greatness of character, for calmness in danger, and for foresight in counsel, that the unanimous result would be that one name alone would be mentioned, and that would be—RAGLAN.

The battle of the Alma affords a proof of the great advantages of attacking a position with troops deployed in successive thin lines. Fearful as was the loss of the light division, it would undoubtedly have been still greater had the advance been made in column; in fact it may be considered doubtful whether any troops in that formation could have stormed such a position. The great front of fire gained by deployment is another advantage; and although the line of the light division had become a good deal broken when they delivered theirs, still it was far superior to that of the enemy, whose crowded encumbered masses could not stand against it, but at once began to give way. A comparatively very small amount of ammunition was fired away by the English in this battle.

The quantity is about as follows :

    Infantry ammunition—90,000 rounds expended.

            Say 15,000 men actually engaged=an average of 6 rounds per man.

    Artillery ammunition—810 rounds expended.

            54 guns in action=an average of 15 rounds per gun.

The accompanying diagram shows the position of the regiments of the light, first, and second divisions, and the number of casualties in each.

There is a remarkable observation of St Arnaud, quoted by De Bazancourt, namely, that our losses were greater than the French, as their troops ran to the attack, whereas ours walked. This, however, can hardly be accepted as true in any sense. The French lost less men simply because it did not fall to their lot to attack the chief position. The heights up which they climbed were so steep, that artillery fire could not in many places be brought effectively against them. Whereas the English advance was up a gradual slope like a glacis, which was swept by artillery throughout. As for the pace at which our men went at it, it was the ordinary march, and by endeavouring to hurry them, more probably would have been lost in steadiness, than would have been gained in time.

De Bazancourt, who, in his account of the battle, also conveys the impression that the chief glory of the day rests with the French troops, and that the conduct of the English was a series of blunders and delays, asserts that the latter were stopped in ascending the heights, and were unable to advance until the French artillery came to the rescue, and by pouring in "*mitraille*" enabled the English to capture the position. It is hardly necessary to say that this account is purely imaginary. No French battery was brought to bear upon the ground attacked by the English. The only artillery in action on that flank, at that time, was the English battery, as already described; and as the heights gained by the French were divided from the chief position attacked by the English, by an amphitheatre a mile wide, the possibility of using "*mitraille*" with effect, at such a range, is put out of the question. He also considers that the victory would have been more complete, had not the English cavalry been stuck in the mud in the marshes of the Alma. This is another purely imaginary idea. Not only the English cavalry, but the troop of horse artillery accompanying them, were at the front at the termination of the battle, and protected the outward flank; but our cavalry took no very active part, as they were a mere handful compared to that of the enemy.*

Lord Raglan has again been accused of inactivity, both by English and French writers, in having remained two days upon the Alma, instead of at once

---

* There are various other misrepresentations and errors in De Bazancourt's book, but they are hardly worth noticing.

advancing in pursuit of the defeated enemy. But there were nearly 2000 wounded Englishmen lying on the field. The sick soon added as many more to the non-effective list. In addition to these, all of whom had to be conveyed two or three miles to the beach and embarked, there were also about 1000 Russian wounded to be cared for, the enemy omitting to send in a flag of truce, or in any way to provide for their own casualties. Our deficiency in means of transport has already been spoken of. The navy on this, as on every occasion, lent their willing assistance, and hundreds of sailors were employed each day in carrying the wounded to the beach, by means of hammocks and cots, slung on spars, &c. But it was a work of time.

How then could Lord Raglan advance until his sick and wounded had been embarked? Could he leave them on the ground uncared for and unprotected? On the other hand, to have left part of his army to guard them, and to have advanced with the other, would have divided his forces, and the strong positions of the Katcha and Belbec were still between him and Sebastopol; and although the defeat at the Alma might be supposed to have disheartened the enemy to a certain extent, there was no reason at the time for supposing them to have been in such a state of panic, as is now represented to have been the case. In judging the conduct of a general it is hardly just to argue upon information obtained after the event, but rather upon that which, in his position at the time, he may have been supposed to have been in possession. As regards the French, it must be borne in mind that their losses were much less than ours, and their contact with the beach afforded them great advantages.

The fact of the English ambulance corps having been left behind at Varna has also been remarked upon. But the extract of Lord Raglan's despatch, already quoted, with respect to the baggage animals, will have explained his difficulties in sea transport. Besides which, the ambulance corps was on a small scale, and created in a hurry when the war began. Its waggons were few in number, heavy and cumbrous in form. The drivers were old pensioners, of whom the sickness at Varna had diminished the already scanty numbers ; so that its means of usefulness, never very great or at all sufficient, had thus been reduced to a minimum before we embarked.

Casualties of the English army at the battle of Alma.

	Killed.	*Wounded.*
Officers	26	73
Men	327	1557
	353	1630
		353

Total 1983

CHAPTER VII.

On the morning of the 23rd of September, the armies again advanced towards Sebastopol. The first day's march brought them to the banks of the river Katcha, where the ground, somewhat similar to that of the Alma, afforded even greater advantages for taking up a defensive position. But the enemy, the traces of whose rapid flight showed how disorganized they had already become after the battle of the 20th, offered no opposition whatever, and the allies on the following day again moved forward, and took up a position on the heights beyond the river Belbec, only a short distance from the head of the harbour of Sebastopol.

It has been generally understood, that the allied commanders in effecting a landing on the coast to the north of the city, had determined in the first instance to proceed to the attack of the large Star fort, which stood on this side of the harbour, and which was the most important work then existing for the defence of the land fronts. The Russians evidently considered

5

this the threatened point and were busy strengthening the works there. A sudden change, however, now occurred in the plans of the allies. It was determined to abandon the north side altogether, and by a flank march to move on Balaclava, gain possession of its harbour, and take up a position in front of the city of Sebastopol itself, which stood on the southern shore.

The original conception of this plan is due to Lord Raglan, who, writing to England from Old Fort, said he thought that " A flank movement to the south side of Sebastopol would be necessary," as he believed the northern forts to be unattackable with the then resources of the allies.

On the day following the battle of the Alma, accordingly, Sir John Burgoyne submitted the following memorandum on the subject :—

Camp on the Alma,
21st September, 1854.

MEMORANDUM. — I would submit that, unless some impeding circumstances occur which cannot now be foreseen, the combined armies should at once move round to the south side of Sebastopol, instead of attacking Fort Constantine; by which the following advantages may be anticipated :

1. That instead of attacking a position naturally strong and of limited extent, to which a powerful support will be given by Fort Constantine, itself a permanent fortification, though by no means formidable

if insulated, the enemy would have to defend a very extensive line divided by vallies, and from every information, very imperfectly, if at all intrenched, and which would probably be forced rapidly.

2. As the advance is from the north, our attack will rather be expected on that side, and not on the south.

3. Even supposing the Fort Constantine to be taken, although it will open the shipping, dockyard, &c. to cannonading, it does not insure entire possession of the important establishments until after a second operation, which may still require to move round to the south, while the enemy will retain to the last free and open communication to the place.

4. There is every reason to believe from the appearance of the maps, and what may be expected to be the formation of the ground, that there is a very strong position between the sea at Balaclava and along the valley of the Chernaya, that would most efficiently cover the allied armies during the operation, but is too extensive to be taken up by the garrison.

5. That the communication with the fleet, which is in fact our base of operations, would be far more secure and commodious by the small harbour of Balaclava, and the bays near Chersonese, than on the open coast to the north, and with the advantage of a good road from Balaclava to the attacks, and a very flat country to pass to them from the bays near Chersonese.

6. Under ordinary circumstances such a movement would have the effect of exposing the communication

of the army to be cut off, but in this case, the idea is, to abandon the communication from the north altogether, and establish a new one to the shipping in the south, which would be moved round for that purpose.

J. F. BURGOYNE,
Lieut.-General.

This proposition appears to have remained undecided for a few days, but on arriving at the Belbec, it was ascertained (as mentioned by Lord Raglan in his despatch afterwards), that at the mouth of that river stood a small fort in possession of the Russians, which although in itself of no great importance, could not be taken without heavy artillery, of which none had been yet landed; at the same time it debarred the use of the mouth of the river for that purpose. To attack and capture this small fort, before commencing on the more important one, would have caused delay. This fact gave additional weight to the able memorandum of Sir John Burgoyne, and the plan was at length adopted by Marshal St. Arnaud.

Subsequent events fully proved the importance and advantage to the allies of this strategic movement, and realized the anticipations expressed in the memorandum.

In going to the south side the following advantages resulted :—

1. A safe harbour and free communication with the fleet.

2. The ground on that side was favourable for defence of the flank.

3. The allies were on the most defenceless side of the harbour, and on which the city docks, stores, &c., and all that gave Sebastopol value, stood.

If they had remained on the north side, they would have had,

1. A strong fort in front.

2. A constant liability to attack in rear when the Russian reinforcements arrived, and the ground, being covered with wood, was unfavourable for defence.

3. There was no harbour at all on the north side, and therefore in any bad weather, all communication with the fleet would have been cut off.

It has been urged that by abandoning their original plan, the allied generals left open the main road to Sebastopol; but as they were not in a condition to make a complete investment, one side must have remained open in either contingency.

In order to strike the main road which leads from the interior of the country down the Mackenzie heights towards Sebastopol and to the plains of Balaclava, the allies, who, on the morning of the 25th September, were on the heights above the Belbec, had for some distance to march in a south-easterly direction through thick woods, in which there was only a slight track for carriages. On the same morning Prince Menschikoff, ignorant of the change, and doubtless conceiving that the plans of the allied

generals were fully decided upon the attack of the
north side, was moving a considerable force by the
same main road up the Mackenzie heights, and into
the country towards Bacshiserai, with the intention,
probably, when his troops had somewhat regained their
confidence, and when they had been joined by reinforcements, to return and attack the Anglo-French
army in its rear.

Thus on the 25th of September the two hostile
forces were unconsciously moving in two lines, which
intersected each other at a point close to the crest of
the heights. Consequently, to the surprise of both,
the advanced guard of the one suddenly found itself
in the presence of the rear guard of the other; and
Lord Raglan, who, as usual, was in front with the
cavalry skirmishers, threading his way through the
thick woods, on coming into the open ground at
Mackenzie's farm almost rode into the carriages and
baggage of the Russian force. Their rear guard, after
standing for a moment, dispersed in the woods on each
side, and part of the English cavalry, with a troop of
horse artillery, pursued for a few miles, capturing a
considerable amount of baggage and some ammunition
waggons on the road.

This casual encounter was so far useful for the moment, that it must have rather mystified the enemy as
to our plans, but Lord Raglan, feeling the importance
of regaining the coast, his army being for the time
scattered for miles along a thin line, at once retraced
his steps and continued his march by the steep road

down the Mackenzie heights : and towards sunset the light and first divisions streamed across the plain and reached the banks of the Chernaya, followed shortly after by the 2nd division. The 3rd division remained for the night on the heights, suffering much from deficiency of water. The French and the 4th division of the English were still in the neighbourhood of the Belbec.

The defence of Balaclava consisted of a small garrison and a battery of four brass mortars, planted in the ruins of the old castle at the mouth of the harbour. When the leading divisions of the English army arrived there on the following morning (26th of September), a few shots were fired as they entered the town, but surrounded on the land side, and shelled by the "Agamemnon" from the sea, the garrison shortly capitulated and were taken prisoners.

The dangerous illness of Marshal St. Arnaud at length obliged him to relinquish his command, and he died a few days afterwards on board ship, on his voyage home. He was succeeded by General Canrobert, a soldier who possessed in a high degree the confidence of the French army.

The events of the campaign had already been sufficient to display some of the great qualities of Lord Raglan's character. It was mainly due to his firmness, supported by that of Sir Edmund Lyons, that the gloomy views entertained at Varna were not allowed to influence the fate of the expedition. The remarkable incident which occurred during the voyage to the Crimea, in displaying the indecision of Marshal St. Arnaud, and his subserviency to the instructions of the Emperor Napoleon, again called forth the resolution of the English Commander-in-chief at a most critical moment.

The choice of the landing-place was mainly determined by Lord Raglan. Again, in the attack of the Russian position at Alma, his clear judgment pronounced against the rashness of an inland movement. The flank march, that one great strategic success of the whole war, was originated and adopted by Lord Raglan, and pressed upon the French commander.

The apparent tardiness of the English on some occasions was owing rather to their unprepared condition for active operations, than to any indifference on the part of Lord Raglan as to the importance of time in war.

In the events that were to follow, it will be found that his character always rose as the danger increased, that he still hoped when others almost despaired, and that his calm undaunted nature regulated the vacillating conduct of the general who succeeded to the command of the French army; and all this at a time when the English nation, misled as to the true facts of the case, and ignorant of the real causes of our misfortunes, withdrew from him their confidence; when the English ministry left him undefended; and when the press vilified and slandered his character, until at length he sank and died of a broken heart.

CHAPTER VIII.

THE fortunate result of the flank march, by giving the allied generals possession of the excellent, though diminutive, harbour of Balaclava, and thus affording them a safe communication with the fleets, relieved them of one of the anxieties hitherto attending their movements, and enabled them to devote all their attention to the one great object of the expedition, the capture of Sebastopol. Accordingly, as the divisions of both armies in succession arrived at Balaclava, they were ordered forward to take position on the great plateau to the south of, and overlooking, the city.

The land defences of Sebastopol* on this side, at the time, consisted on the east of a round masonry tower, built on commanding ground and mounting four guns (the Malakoff), and on the west, of a crenelated wall terminated by another tower, overlooking the Quarantine harbour ; and between these, at one or

* See general plan at the end.

two intermediate points, were a few earthworks not completed, and apparently not armed. These defences were certainly not of a very formidable description, or likely to afford a lengthened defence; indeed so slight were they considered by some, that the idea of immediate assault suggested itself, and was even advocated by officers of high rank. Such an attempt had many attractions; the defences appeared so slight, and the enemy's troops were known to be disorganized and in alarm. On the other hand, the garrison was almost equal in strength to the allies; the approaches were commanded by guns, which, though few in number, were of heavy calibre; and the enemy had placed line-of-battle ships to sweep the several ravines which led down to the place.

To attempt then to assault so large a garrison, partially intrenched, protected by artillery and by the guns of a powerful fleet, was a most hazardous venture. To attempt it and to fail, would have been a serious misfortune at a moment when large reinforcements of the enemy were known to be on their way. Moreover, as the allies had two powerful siege trains on board ship close at hand, it was considered rash to run the risk of a reverse, when it was not doubted that after a bombardment of heavy artillery the assault might be made with a certainty of success. That the enemy would profit, as they did, by the interval of delay, and would suddenly display such energy and perseverance in strengthening their works, and in making use of the unlimited means afforded by a great arsenal and dockyard, nothing in their conduct hitherto had given reason to suppose.

In taking up their ground before Sebastopol, had the original order of march of the allies been preserved, the French would have been on the right and the English on the left of the position; but the latter having possession of Balaclava, and the former having in like manner found Kamiesch a convenient harbour, it was decided that the armies should respectively change places.

In order to guard the exposed flank, two divisions of the French army, with some thousand Turks under General Bosquet, were encamped along the edge of the plateau, overlooking the valley of the Chernaya. The relative proportions of the French and English armies, in point of numbers, were already much changed since the first landing. The French had received large reinforcements, while the effective strength of the English had become reduced by sickness and losses in action.

On the 28th September the disembarkation of the English siege train commenced at Balaclava harbour. Its details were as follows :

* 8-Inch Guns——20 ⎱
  24-Pr. Guns ——30 ⎰ With 500 rounds per gun.

15-Inch Mortars—10   With 300 rounds per mortar.

———

60

* Four of these were Lancaster guns with elliptical bores, and with a small amount of extra ammunition.

1000 seamen and 50 naval guns of large calibre were also landed; but only a small proportion of the latter were placed in position in the first instance.

Nothing could exceed the enthusiasm both of the gunners and sailors in their exertions to forward this great siege train to the heights in readiness to be placed in position. But here again the want of transport was severely felt; the few arabas which had been captured in the country, drawn by oxen and camels, were totally unsuited for the carriage of the enormous weights of modern armaments. The horses and stripped waggons of the field artillery were therefore employed; but the constant alarms on the flank, and the battles which speedily followed, rendered them liable at any moment to be called away for their more legitimate occupation. Pack ponies were also employed to carry up the shot and shell in sacks.

In the mean time the Russians were indefatigable in their exertions, and every hour added to the strength of their works. A rampart of earth was thrown up round the Malakoff tower, and another work in front of the English (the Redan), grew more formidable daily, both mounting heavy guns. Lord Raglan in his despatch of the 18th October, describes the position of the enemy as being "that of an intrenched camp on very strong ground, where an apparently unlimited number of heavy guns, amply provided with gunners and ammunition, are mounted." They were profuse in the expenditure of shot and shell. A solitary individual could scarcely show himself, even at extreme range, without at once attracting notice from the ships or batteries.

From Sebastopol the ground rose gradually, attaining its greatest height at about 3000 yards from the place, and the investing armies were encamped just beyond the crest. The ground was also intersected by several steep and rocky ravines, running down towards the city, and terminating in the various creeks and bays on the south side of the great fort. These features were most strongly developed in front of the English position.

The first aspect of the defences of Sebastopol pointed to the Malakoff tower as the key of the whole position, as it commanded both the city and the anchorage, and it seemed probable, therefore, that the possession of this work by the allies would involve the fall of the whole place. This was at once perceived by Sir John Burgoyne, who accordingly proposed that the operations should be confined to this side of the town; that batteries should be established against the Malakoff, either upon the mound known afterwards as the " Mamelon " (at a distance of about 600 yards), or upon other convenient ground in that direction; and that meanwhile the enemy should be held in check on the left, and Kamiesch guarded, by a French corps.

A memorandum of Sir John Burgoyne's dated 29th September, 1854, thus speaks of the Malakoff tower:—
" On the right the great tower appears to be the key of the whole position, and the only work to prevent

an assault at any time.   A good site or sites for not less than eight guns, of which one or two, at most, shell guns, must be sought for to demolish that tower." * * Again—"There is a plateau exactly opposite the tower,* which is well situated to batter it from, but it seems to be somewhat nearer than is desirable, and what is of more consequence, it is rocky: it is to be hoped some more convenient situation may be found, but it will be necessary that the guns see very clearly as low down as the line of loop-holes.   On the green hill, probably, two batteries of four shell guns each, may greatly destroy the two faces of the redoubt† by oblique fire." *   *   *

Instead of the proposed plan against the Malakoff, however, that of the French General was adopted; namely, to make the bastion-du-mât the chief point of attack, and to open regular .trenches and batteries opposite its salient (see plan).   By this arrangement the English attack became, as it were, subservient to, and supporting the right of, the French, and its batteries were accordingly constructed with a view to a general bombardment of the works in its front (viz. the Malakoff, Redan, and Barrack batteries, and the ships in the various creeks, but without the intention of prosecuting regular approaches.

On the night of the 9th October the French opened their trenches against the place, at about 900 yards distance, followed on the 10th and 11th by the Eng-

---

* Called afterwards the "Mamelon."

† Called afterwards the great Redan.

lish, at distances ranging from 1400 to 1500 yards.

The configuration and rocky nature of the ground were causes of the great distance from the place at which the English batteries were constructed, a disadvantage partially redeemed by the powerful nature of their ordnance. But there was another important circumstance which influenced their position, and prevented their being as close as was desirable. As the French attack on the left had been decided upon as the principal one, the main body of their army was drawn in that direction for their purpose of carrying it out. The ground thus remaining on the right for English occupation was so considerable, and our numbers, always inadequate, were already so reduced, that it was found impossible to cover it altogether, or to extend sufficiently to form a complete investment. Consequently our position on the extreme right terminated suddenly on the high ground overlooking Inkermann; and between this point and the head of the harbour the Russians held possession, so much so, that convoys passed in and out of the city.

In opening our trenches, therefore, it was necessary to consider this circumstance, and rather to *refuse the right*, that is, withdraw that flank, or the enemy would have been actually in rear of our batteries. It is important to bear in mind the circumstance of our weakness in numbers in this direction, because it led subsequently to an attack there by the enemy, on the great day of Inkermann.

By indefatigable exertions, the trenches, in spite of the rocky nature of the ground, were rapidly completed and armed on the night of the 14th, 15th, and 16th October. The morning of the 17th accordingly was fixed upon for the opening of the bombardment.

It will be apparent from what has been said, that two results were contingent upon the opening of fire ; namely :

1. The fall of the whole of the south side by a general assault, after a few hours' cannonade. Or :

2. The possession by the French at all events of the bastion-du-mât.

The first was doubtless the one confidently expected ; and the following are extracts from Lord Raglan's instructions issued on the occasion : —

The fire upon Sebastopol to commence at half-past 6 a.m.,* from the French and English batteries in coöperation with the allied fleets. The signal to be the discharge of three mortars by the French.

The troops off duty (that is, not in the trenches) to be ready to fall in at a moment's notice.

Horses of the field batteries to be harnessed. One officer of engineers and 20 sappers, with picks, shovels, crowbars, and bags of powder, to be ready to accompany each division.

One officer of artillery and 20 gunners, with rockets and spikes, to be ready to accompany each division. Advanced piquets, except men selected to fire into the

* On the 17th of October.

embrasures, to be withdrawn. The troops at Balaclava to be on the alert.

Lord Raglan will be at the quarries in front of the
3rd division. General Canrobert will be at the maison
d'eau.

The following is the armament of the English and
French batteries.

English	Right attack .	7 32-Prs . . 6 24-Prs . . 8 8-Inch guns 5 10-Inch mortars	Directed against the Malakoff tower, the Redan, Barrack batteries, ship in dock-yard creek, and bastion-du mât. The mortars to shell the dockyard, &c.
	Left attack . .	24 24-Prs . . 12 8-Inch guns 5 10-Inch mortars	
	Lancaster battery	4 68-Prs . .	Against Malakoff, ships, &c.
	Piquet House battery	1 Lancaster gun . .	Against ship in creek, &c.

Total   72, of which 42 were manned by
Royal Artillery, and 30 by
Naval Brigade.

French	43 guns 10 mortars	Chiefly directed against the bastion-du-mât.

53

Having in view the objects just specified, and in
order as far as possible to insure success in so critical

and important an operation, Lord Raglan and General
Canrobert most earnestly requested Admirals Dundas
and Hamelin, respectively commanding the allied
fleets, to coöperate by simultaneously attacking the
sea defences.

Vice-Admiral Dundas, it is known, was opposed to
this plan; conceiving:

1. That as the line of sunken Russian ships and
the boom across the mouth of the harbour prevented
his entering, he could, therefore, only bombard from a
distance the forts on each side, there not being sufficient space or even depth of water to take the men-
of-war into close quarters, without causing one to
mask the fire of the other.

2. That a distant bombardment would be in-
effectual upon the forts, at the same time that their
fire in return might be very damaging to the allied
fleets.

3. That, therefore, a great risk would be incurred of
crippling the allied fleets, without the prospect of a
compensating advantage; whereas, the enemy had
still a powerful squadron of 11 line-of-battle ships
and 11 frigates and war steamers in the harbour.

The occasion, however, was momentous; and it was
considered that the naval bombardment would necessarily distract the garrison, and oblige them to withdraw part of their force from the land fronts, and that
the ships would also prove so powerful a support to
the left flank of the French, that it was finally decided
to carry out the plan. Indeed the French Admiral,

according to the rules of their service, being bound to obey the orders of the Commander-in-chief on land, had no option, and Admiral Dundas therefore acquiesced. It had been arranged that the attack by sea should be made by the men-of-war whilst in movement, each delivering its fire in succession, but this also was altered, and the three combined fleets during the bombardment were anchored across the mouth of the harbour.

CHAPTER IX.

THE FIRST BOMBARDMENT.—17th October, 1854.

GENERAL CANROBERT, a man of great apparent energy and ardent temperament, suddenly placed at the head of a magnificent army, and at a moment when the prestige of success seemed to add to its strength, and to render it almost invincible, entertained most sanguine hopes of the immediate fall of the place, and in spite of the vigour which had latterly been displayed by the enemy, there were few at that moment in the allied armies, or perhaps even in Sebastopol, who doubted the result.

It was a beautiful morning when the French and English batteries suddenly opened, at about half-past 6 a.m., on the 17th October. The Russians, although taken by surprise at first, quickly returned the fire, which became furious on all sides. Notwithstanding the long range, the heavy metal of the English batteries soon began to tell: in a couple of hours the four guns on the top of the Malakoff tower were silenced and overthrown, never to be mounted again. The earthen batteries round it, as also those of the Redan and Barrack battery, however, kept up a steady cannonade.

The French siege guns, made of brass, being of lighter calibre, and at closer quarters, were less rapid in their fire, and soon felt severely the weight of their antagonists. At about half-past 9 a.m., a magazine in one of their principal batteries unfortunately exploded, which silenced its fire and caused 100 casualties, followed soon after by a second explosion. Their remaining batteries, partially enfiladed, and totally overpowered, were consequently unable to continue the combat, and at half-past 10 a.m., by order of General Canrobert, ceased firing. The enemy having thus obtained the mastery in one direction, directed all their efforts against the British batteries, which, however, as stated by Lord Raglan in his despatch, " kept up an unremitting fire throughout the day; to his own and the general satisfaction, as well as to the admiration of the French army." At about 3 p.m. a terrific explosion took place inside the Redan, and for some time after not a gun opened from it.

In the mean time, at about 1 p.m., the allied fleets commenced their attack on the sea front; that of the English being opposed to the north forts at a range of about 1200 or 1500 yards; the nearest ships (the Agamemnon and Sanspareil) being about 800 yards from Fort Constantine. The Turkish fleet was in the centre, and the French attacked the quarantine and southern forts, but at long range.

The position of the ships is shown in the plan.

The object, however, for which their coöperation had
been so urgently desired, had already been frustrated
by the untoward accidents in the French trenches.
The assault of the land fronts, which had been intended, could not now be attempted, and in fact the
enemy had the boldness during the afternoon to make
a sortie against the French which was quickly repulsed.

The fleets, therefore, after remaining in action for
some hours, drew off towards sunset, having suffered
rather considerably.

Their casualties were about as follows:

$$\left.\begin{matrix} \text{English—44} \\ \text{French—32} \end{matrix}\right\} \text{Killed.} \qquad \left.\begin{matrix} 266 \\ 180 \end{matrix}\right\} \text{Wounded.}$$

The casualties in Sebastopol on the 17th of October
as stated by Prince Menschikoff were:

Killed . . . . Admiral Korniloff.

Wounded . . Admiral Nachimoff.

Killed and Wounded . . . . 500.

Fort Constantine "much damaged." Magazine in
Redan exploded, and almost all its guns (33) dis-
mounted.

As Prince Menschikoff also states that the English
batteries were silenced that evening, with the exception of two guns, it may be as well to add an extract
from the report of the officers in the trenches.

Result of the first day's fire:

$$\text{English Batteries}\left\{\begin{matrix} \text{1 Gun burst . . . Lancaster.} \\ \text{5 Gun carriages . Disabled} \\ \text{5 Platforms . . . Ditto} \\ \text{2 Gunwheels . . Ditto} \end{matrix}\right. \left.\begin{matrix} \\ \end{matrix}\right\} \begin{matrix} \text{Repaired} \\ \text{during the} \\ \text{night.} \end{matrix}$$

But the mere calculation of casualties will afford no criterion of the important consequences that ensued from the bombardment of the 17th of October, or of the altered position of the allies. Neither of the anticipated results had been realized, and it became evident that the artillery of the enemy was far more numerous and powerful than had been at all supposed; that their resources were immense, and their determination unflinching. The evident inferiority in metal of the French artillery, the certainty that the enemy could repair damages, replenish their batteries, and mount fresh guns, far quicker than the allies could hope to do, with all their material miles distant : all these considerations proved that the hope of an immediate and successful assault could no longer be entertained, and that even the possession of the bastion-du-mât was a distant and doubtful speculation.

Mortifying as these results were, and a gloomy answer to the bright hopes of the morning, still even these were not the worst conditions which the crisis presented. The enemy were safe behind intrenchments which every hour increased in strength, and great reinforcements of troops were daily expected. The allies, on the contrary, were weak in numbers, limited in means, and the winter which was approaching would find them on an exposed plateau, without shelter, and with open trenches. Added to this, the cholera still decimated their ranks, and in the English army alone the average diminution from sickness was about 100 men daily.   3000 were already in hospitals at Scutari !

Judging from his published despatches, General Canrobert did not at this time take so gloomy a view of the position.   Writing a few days after, he states that his means of attack were concentrated on the bastion-du-mât, and that, assisted by the English, he hoped soon to gain possession of it.   Again on the 22nd, he is sanguine ; but speaks of his difficulties being two-fold—1st, the nature of the soil—2nd, the number and weight of the enemy's artillery.

Lord Raglan, however, did not conceal his apprehensions ; for on the 23rd he writes, that the fire of the enemy is not seriously diminished ; that with ˙plenty of men, and unlimited resources, they are able to repair their works, re-mount guns, and reöpen fire from batteries which had been silenced ; and that, consequently, he is unable to say when ulterior measures may be undertaken.   In fact, the exhaustion of the allies was now but a matter of time.   In the first twenty-four hours, the English had expended 100 rounds per gun ; and although by borrowing ammunition from the fleet, and by firing more slowly, the bombardment might be prolonged, still the fire of the enemy grew more vigorous as ours relaxed ; and should no assault be made, in a few days, more or less, the contest must close, by the exhaustion of ammunition, the wearing out of the guns, to say nothing of the physical prostration of the gunners from over-work.

Such, then, were the grave consequences which gradually became apparent, after the opening of the bombardment on the 17th of October. Our want of success on that day arose principally from two causes :

1. The light calibre of the French siege guns.

2. The explosion of one of their principal magazines.

The first may be explained by the consideration, that neither in France, nor in England, was apprehended the necessity of any overpowering armament to reduce a place, which, so far as its land defence went, was not supposed to present great difficulties. The second was an unfortunate contretemps.

Lord Raglan spent the whole of the 17th in the quarries, in front of the 3rd division, whence he obtained a complete panoramic view of the position, and from whence he had hoped in the afternoon to lead his troops to the assault. Speaking some months afterwards of this day, he stated his opinion, that the great explosion in the Redan should have been the signal for assault; that the place had never, before or since, been so prostrate as at that moment; but that, of course, in the then condition of the French batteries it was out of the question to attempt it.

The following extracts from an article published

afterwards in the "Moniteur," give a clear summary of this first part of the siege.

"The Anglo-French army was not, in fact, numerous enough to make a complete investment. It was, therefore, necessary to limit it to an attack of the south side. To accomplish this operation the English took possession of the port of Balaclava. The French, seeking a point d'appui on the shore to land their provisions and artillery, providentially found the port of Kamiesch. * * * "

"Sebastopol, as is known, is not surrounded by battlements; it is rather a great intrenched camp, containing generally an army of from 15,000 to 20,000 men, already protected at the commencement of the siege by numerous earth batteries; and especially by the Russian fleet, which, well placed in the inner port, could bear upon all the avenues by which the allies could advance upon the place. At this period, that is to say, when the Anglo-French army had arrived before Sebastopol, the assault might perhaps have been attempted; but it was already a hazardous enterprise, without sufficient artillery to silence that of the enemy."

"Doubtless nothing was impossible to an Anglo-French army." * * * *

"But success alone could justify so daring an attempt. The first duty imposed by the responsibility of command is prudence: and prudence pre-

scribed to the Commanders-in-chief not to attempt
the assault with at most an army of 50,000 men,
placed on a rock, deficient of artillery or ammunition reserves, without being defended by intrenchments in the rear, and with no other refuge but
the ships. It would have been risking on one
cast the fortune and fate of the expedition, and
nothing must be risked at a distance of 800
leagues from the mother country."

"The coup-de-main, which the generals thought
possible after the battle of the Alma, having
escaped them, there only remained for them a
regular siege according to the rules of military
art. At the very outset the Russians took two
most efficacious measures, very regrettable for us.
The first was Prince Menschikoff's strategic move,
who, instead of shutting himself up in Sebastopol,
marched on Simpheropol and kept the field and
free communication with the besieged city. The
second was the energetic decision of sinking a
portion of the men-of-war, which rendered the enemy's port inaccessible to our fleets, and gave
some 500 or 600 guns with their sailors as
gunners to assist in the defence of the town.
Thus, although the town already presented a formidable row of guns, new batteries rose as if by
enchantment, and our feeble siege artillery could
not master the fire of the town. From this moment it became evident to all, that Sebastopol
could only be taken after a long struggle, with

powerful reinforcements, at the cost perhaps of sanguinary battles." * * * *

The altered position of the allies, as described, did not perhaps become so immediately or generally apparent. With a furious bombardment still being carried on; with the energy and activity displayed by the French, who reöpened fire on the morning of the 19th, with good effect, and who constantly pushed forward their trenches, and opened fresh batteries, there seemed still a prospect of final success. The English, too, feeling that all their hopes rested on the French attack, fought with unequalled courage and skill to endeavour to subdue the enemy's fire. Their nights were passed in replenishing with ammunition, and repairing damages. A new battery was opened by them on the right of the French trenches to sweep the dockyard creek. The suburbs were constantly set on fire in different places by hot shot, rockets, and shells. As the guns first mounted became disabled, they were replaced by others of heavier calibre.

Lord Raglan spent many hours daily in carefully watching the effect, but without being able to arrive at any satisfactory conclusion. On the 23rd of October a special report of the actual state of the batteries, and of the amount of ammunition remaining, was made to him, and again on the 29th. The hour of their exhaustion was rapidly approaching. General Canrobert, still anticipating success, but dangerously slow in making up his mind for an assault, speaks on the 27th of October (in his despatch) of the construction of new batteries, and on the 1st of November opens his third parallel at 140 metres from the salient of the bastion-du-mât.

Had Sebastopol been a city regularly fortified, and with only limited means, and had it been invested, this gradual progress would have been satisfactory, and in time conclusive; but under the actual conditions, the only chance of the allies was a crushing fire, followed by an overwhelming assault at various points. The enemy, however, strengthened by the arrival of reinforcements, and foreseeing that some attempt of the kind must ensue in a few days, endeavoured to prevent, or at all events delay it, by themselves assuming the offensive on the exposed flank.

It must be understood that already the original equality of the French and English armies, in point of numbers, as landed in the Crimea, had disappeared; the French now amounting to about 35,000, and the English infantry not much exceeding 16,000 men; and these proportions of inequality became far greater as the siege progressed.

The following details will be sufficiently explanatory of the progress of the bombardment, for the few days preceding the battle of Balaclava.

18th October .. { Heavy firing from English and Russian batteries. The French silent. Alarm at Balaclava.

19th October .	French and English batteries firing vigorously. Russians a good deal damaged. The town set on fire with hot shot.
20th ditto	Another explosion in the French trenches ; their fire slack.
20th ditto	The Russians make a sortie against the French, and spike some mortars. A new English 3-gun battery (Piquet House) commenced on the right of the French lines, to enfilade the creek, &c.
21st ditto	The English suffer from the fire of the Garden batteries. The French open their 2nd parallel.
22nd ditto	24-Pr. gun burst. Firing ordered to be slower, viz. 75 rounds per gun, per diem.
23rd ditto	Progress unsatisfactory. Gunners much fatigued. Many guns disabled.
24th ditto	Piquet House (3-gun) battery opened : Russian fire still heavy.

The English fired little at night, being constantly engaged in repairing their batteries and platforms, mounting fresh guns, sending down ammunition, shot and shell, &c. The Russians were also evidently occupied in the same manner, as was apparent by their vigour each morning. As the bombardment progressed, the English guns and carriages became much shaken and knocked about. The Russians constantly constructed new works, and opened fresh batteries.

CHAPTER X.

LEAVING the siege to its ever-varying yet still monotonous alternations of progress and disappointment, to its sickening hopes and increasing feebleness, we must now turn to the consideration of the ground on the exposed flank, from Balaclava to Inkermann, in which direction the enemy, by means of strong diversions, hoped to delay, if not altogether avert, the threatened capture of their city.

The harbour of Balaclava, surrounded by precipitous hills, presented on its eastern side close to the sea no great difficulties for defence (see general plan). The ground was so abrupt and lofty, that a few earthen batteries (marked A. B. C. D. and E.) with guns of position, and a force of 1000 Marines, rendered it tolerably safe, except from a surprise. The guns in the battery A. swept the only approach in that direction, which was by a mountain path. Nevertheless this point was one to be jealously watched, as the enemy in possession of the " Marine heights " would have rendered Balaclava untenable.*   From the head of the harbour, stretching away to the north-east towards the river Chernaya, was a large undulating plain which, as presenting less natural means of defence, was a point more liable to attack.   Some of the batteries already named on the heights gave a flanking fire in this direction, as also one (marked F.) on rising ground in front of the village of Kadikoi, where the 93rd regiment of Highlanders were stationed.   The English cavalry were encamped in the plain between Kadikoi and the ridge of the plateau, on which stood Bosquet's corps.

Considering the immense importance of Balaclava, as the only depôt of the English army, and considering its isolated position, it being several miles from the plateau, these means of defence will appear scarcely sufficient or satisfactory.   But Lord Raglan, with the great bulk of his diminished army in front of Sebastopol, could not afford to detach a larger force to guard his flank.   Over-worked, enfeebled, their numbers were far too few in both directions.

At about 2000 yards in advance of the village of Kadikoi on the plain, was a low range of hillocks, which extended in a sort of curve from the foot of the great plateau under Bosquet's corps, almost to the village of Kamara; that nearest the latter being the

* Guns of position at Balaclava Fort . . .
$$\left\{ \begin{array}{l} \left. \begin{array}{l} A-2 \\ B-6 \end{array} \right\} \text{guns} \\ \left. \begin{array}{l} C \\ D \\ E \\ F \end{array} \right\} \text{5 guns each} \end{array} \right\} \text{With 100 rounds per gun.}$$

7

most commanding.   On these, by way of strengthening the position, several battalions of Turks were dis-
tributed, who at once commenced constructing redoubts (marked* 1, 2, 3, 4, 5, 6, in plan), some of
which during the month of October were armed with
English iron 12-Prs. manned by Turkish gunners.   It
had been originally intended that these redoubts
should be armed with Turkish guns, and which were
landed from their fleets at Kameisch Bay for this purpose ; but the great distance to transport them, the
want of means, and their cumbersome and antiquated
form, induced Lord Raglan to lend English guns, of
which the enemy unfortunately deprived them a few
days after.   Although this exterior line of defence was
no doubt at too great a distance from Balaclava, its
adoption was almost imperative, as this range of small
hills, if left unoccupied, would have enabled the enemy
to concentrate large forces unseen, and dangerously
near to the town ; further, it was represented that the
Turkish soldiers fought stoutly behind intrenchments ;
and although their conduct on the 25th somewhat
deceived expectation in this respect, still it must be
stated that the redoubts were not then completed, nor
were the ditches sufficiently deep.   Lord Raglan
constantly expressed great anxiety about this exterior
line of defences, especially, as regards No. 1 fort

* Guns in the Turk-
ish Redoubts . . . .
$\left.\begin{array}{l} \text{No. 1, 3 Iron 12-Prs.} \\ \text{No. 2, 2 \quad ,,} \\ \text{No. 3, 2 \quad ,,} \\ \text{No. 4, 2 \quad ,,} \end{array}\right\}$ English.

which was the most important; and he gave the Turkish soldiers every assistance, in the hopes of being able to render that part of the position secure, before the arrival of Russian reinforcements. It was at his urgent demand that 300 Turkish gunners were landed to man the guns in these forts ; and a few English artillery-men were also sent there to instruct in the details of the guns lent to them.

The chief communication from Balaclava to the plateau, was by a road which passed through Kadikoi, and then ascended by a long gradual rise to the " col " (vide plan). From this latter point to Inkermann (a distance of several miles), the plateau was abruptly terminated by a slope which descended for some hundred feet to the plain, and on the crest of which, as already stated, stood Bosquet's corps. With the exception of the Woronzoff road, this part of the position was safe from any attack accompanied by artillery throughout its length, and it was further strengthened by General Bosquet with occasional forts and guns of position, so that it might be considered impregnable.

Such was the nature of the ground, and of the defences, on the flank of the allied position. The only weak points were at its two extremities, Balaclava and Inkermann. The enemy attacked us at both in succession.

Position and strength of the allied armies before the battle of Balaclava :—·

English before Sebastopol, and at Inkermann, about	15,000
English at Balaclava, 93rd regiment, Marines, and sick depôt	2,000
Turkish forts at Balaclava . . .	2,000
French corps de siege—Three divisions under General Forey	25,000*
French corps of observation,— Two divisions, and Turks, under General Bosquet . . .	15,000

Total   59,000

In order to arrive at a correct appreciation of the battles of Balaclava and Inkermann, it is necessary to observe carefully these numbers, and the respective position of the allied armies, on the map.

BATTLE OF BALACLAVA.

The enemy had been observed for some days hovering in the neighbourhood of Balaclava, and the troops there were kept constantly on the alert. The first reinforcement for Prince Menschikoff's army having arrived, on the morning of the 25th of October at daylight, General Liprandi with 20,000 infantry, supported by a strong force of cavalry, and about 40 guns, made a determined attack upon our flank at

* De Bazancourt.

this point.   The battle commenced by an assault of
the Turkish redoubt on Canrobert's hill.   (No. 1 in
plan.)   This was well defended by the garrison for
some time, but was finally captured, 150* Turks being
killed, and three guns taken in it.   The Turkish troops
in the forts Nos. 2 and 3, seeing those in the first
defeated, evacuated their position without attempting
defence, and retreated in disorder across the plain, in
spite of the support afforded them by the Earl of
Lucan, with the English cavalry and a troop of horse
artillery, which latter, as well as a battery from
Kadikoi, was in action between the forts. The garrison
of No. 4 also speedily followed the example of the
others.   The gunners of the Royal Artillery, who had
been lent to the Turks for the purposes of instruction, spiked the guns in each fort when the Turks
evacuated.

The enemy had thus somewhat easily possessed
themselves of four forts, capturing in them nine
English 12-pounder iron guns, some tents, and ammunition, &c., and prepared, after a slight delay, for
a still more serious attack on the inner line of defences.
Their cavalry, consisting both of regulars and Cossacks,
advanced rapidly and with great boldness across the
plain.   About four hundred detaching themselves
from the main body, charged towards the 93rd Highlanders who were in line in front of Kadikoi (having
some of the defeated Turks on either flank).   The
latter again gave way on the approach of the enemy ;

* General Liprandi's despatch.

but the Russian cavalry finding themselves received with perfect steadiness by the Highlanders, and fired upon by some of the batteries from the "Marine heights," and also by a field battery near Kadikoi, did not pursue the attack in this direction.

In the mean time the main body bore down towards the English cavalry. The latter, when the Turks evacuated the outer line of defence, had fallen back nearly to their own encampment, so as to afford support to the flank of Sir Colin Campbell's force, and also to give clear range to his guns. Lord Lucan, who was commanding, then received orders from Lord Raglan to detach eight squadrons of heavy cavalry still nearer to Balaclava. It was at the moment when this was being executed that the Russians were seen advancing, and the charge which followed is described by the Earl of Lucan, in a speech subsequently made in the House of Lords, as follows:

"The heavy dragoons had already proceeded some distance, when I perceived through the orchard that a body of Russian cavalry was coming over the hill. I rode at speed, and just succeeded in joining the leading squadrons of Greys and Enniskillen dragoons as they were rounding the orchard, and had only time to wheel them into line, and to order an immediate charge under General Scarlett. The enemy was advancing in a dense column, with their flanks protected by two wings; these, so soon as they found that they out-flanked my four squadrons, wheeled about inwards and totally enveloped them; on which I attacked them with the 5th Dragoon Guards in the rear, and in flank with the 4th Dragoon Guards, when the whole mass of the enemy, amounting to at least 3500 men, was repulsed and routed by eight small squadrons of about 700 men—only one-fifth of their number."***

The retreat of the Russians was still further hasten-ed by the fire of two troops of horse artillery; and had the English light cavalry (who were at no great distance during the charge) attacked them at the time in flank, they would have been still more roughly handled. Lord Raglan, who was standing on the heights, and could see the whole distinctly, states in his despatch, that the charge was one of the most suc-cessful he had ever witnessed; the result was never for a moment doubtful, and was in the highest degree creditable to General Scarlett and the officers and men engaged in it.

It was made at a very important moment, and com-pletely checked the movements of the enemy, whose infantry, previous to the charge, had been advancing, but who after the retreat of their cavalry, showed no further disposition to attack Balaclava, and remained inactive and partially concealed behind the ridge of the forts they had captured.

Another short pause now took place, during which it will be necessary to consider the respective positions of the opposed armies. The main body of the Rus-sians was at a considerable distance, at the extremity of the plain near the Chernaya. Their right, thrown forward with artillery, rested on the Fedhukine heights; their left was also much in advance, with cavalry and artillery concentrated behind the forts. It will thus be understood that their position formed three sides of a square.

Meanwhile, in compliance with orders received as soon as the attack had commenced, the first and fourth divisions of the English army had left their camp before Sebastopol, and soon after the heavy cavalry charge were marching from the "col" down to the valley of Balaclava.

Lord Raglan, wishing to recover the Turkish forts, now despatched the following orders:

1. To the Earl of Lucan — "The cavalry to advance and take advantage of every opportunity to recover the heights. They will be supported by infantry which has been ordered to advance on two fronts."

2. To Sir George Cathcart—To the effect that he was to proceed with the 4th division along the ridge of the Turkish forts, and re-capture the whole in succession.

3. To the Duke of Cambridge—To proceed in the direction of Balaclava with the 1st division, and to advance from that point on the Turkish redoubts.

Lord Lucan, on receipt of his order, moved the light cavalry to the outer valley beyond the Turkish forts, and the heavy cavalry on to the ridge near fort No. 5, and there halted (see plan). The two infantry divisions continued their march. According to Lord Raglan's despatch, and in a letter written by him on the subject afterwards, his order to Lord Lucan did not seem to have been attended to; a delay occurred, and the object was not accomplished. The enemy seeing fresh troops coming down from the "col," and probably expecting an attack, were now observed attempting to remove the guns they had captured. Doubts have been expressed whether this was actually the case, but, as when No. 4 fort was a short time afterwards re-taken by Sir George Cathcart, its two English guns were found outside and upset in the ditch, it would certainly appear that something of the kind was taking place. The two English infantry divisions had by this time arrived in the valley.

Lord Raglan now sent another written order by Captain Nolan to Lord Lucan, and which was as follows :—" Lord Raglan wishes the cavalry to advance rapidly to the front, follow the enemy, and try to prevent them carrying away the guns. Troop of horse artillery may accompany. French cavalry on your left. Immediate."

The fair construction of the orders, which were thus issued by Lord Raglan, would appear to be, that Lord Lucan was to hang upon the retreating enemy, ready to recover the heights or the guns as opportunities might offer, using for the purpose all the cavalry at his disposal, and the horse artillery; and that he was to be supported by the two divisions of infantry.

What followed on the receipt of the last order is thus related by the Earl of Lucan in a letter to Lord Raglan dated 30th November :—

" After carefully reading this order, I hesitated, and urged the uselessness of such an attack, and the dangers attending it. The aide-de-camp, in a most authoritative tone, stated that they were Lord Raglan's orders, that the cavalry should attack immediately. I asked, ' Where, and what to do ? ' neither enemy nor guns being in sight. He replied in a most disrespectful but significant manner, pointing to the further end of the valley, ' There, my lord, is your enemy ; there are your guns.' So distinct, in my opinion, was your written instruction, and so positive and urgent were the orders delivered by the aide-de-camp, that I felt it was imperative on me to obey, and I informed Lord Cardigan that he was to advance, and to the objections he made, and in which I entirely agreed, I replied that the order was from your lordship. Having decided, against my conviction, to make the movement, I did all in my power to render it as little perilous as possible. I formed the brigade in two lines, and led to its support two regiments of heavy cavalry, the Scots Greys and Royals, and only halted them when they had reached the point from which they could protect the retreat of the light cavalry, in the event of their being pursued by the enemy ; and when, having already lost many officers and men by the fire from the batteries and fort, any further advance would have exposed them to destruction." * * * *

The subject of this charge has been much discussed, and opinions vary ; if the facts, as now related, are correct, it will perhaps, therefore, be better to leave them to the judgment of the reader, than to make comments upon them. As it was, the light cavalry (formed as shown in the diagram) advanced down the

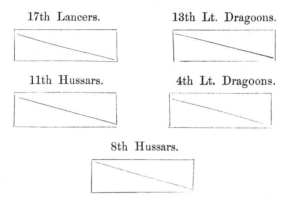

17th Lancers.   13th Lt. Dragoons.

11th Hussars.   4th Lt. Dragoons.

8th Hussars.

outer valley. They did not attempt to attack the enemy who was behind the Turkish forts; they did not attempt to intercept the English guns which were being withdrawn; but they rode steadily down to death. Artillery opened upon them on their right as they passed, also upon their left from the Fedhukine heights, and in front from the main body of the Russian army.

A charge of this kind is probably unsurpassed in the annals of war. We have heard of 400 young soldiers standing quietly on parade on the deck of the Birkenhead steamer as she sank, and numberless instances might be given of the gallantry and devotion of British soldiers; but the steady advance of 500 men to almost certain death, is a perfect marvel of discipline and heroic courage. Suffering fearfully from the fire poured upon them in three directions, they at length rushed through the enemy's guns, cut down the gunners, passed beyond them, and attacked cavalry in the rear, but, " assailed by artillery, infantry, and cavalry," they at length retired.   That any should return from that fearful ride seems only a wonder.

The gallant conduct of the Chasseurs d' Afrique deserves especial mention.   Formed on the left of the light cavalry, as the latter advanced to the charge, the Chasseurs rushed upon the artillery of the enemy, stationed on the Fedhukine heights, turned their flank, and put their gunners to the sword ; thus making an important diversion in which they suffered rather severely.

Meanwhile, Sir George Cathcart with the 4th division advanced along the ridge, and re-captured without difficulty the fort No. 4, outside of which its two 12-pounder guns were found lying spiked and upset.   Subsequently the field battery of the 4th division, together with two others that had arrived from before Sebastopol, shelled the enemy, who still retained possession of the more distant forts, but no further advance was made by Sir George Cathcart.

Lord Raglan, who had been joined by General Canrobert, seeing that the enemy were showing a disposition to retire across the Chernaya, was still anxious to advance upon them with the troops then in the plain, which now consisted of two English and one French divisions of infantry, the English cavalry, and 36 field guns ; but General Canrobert objected, on the principle, that as the capture of Sebastopol was the main object, no risk should be incurred at other points.

With respect to the permanent defence of Balaclava, as the means at Lord Raglan's disposal had proved inadequate to hold so extensive a position as had been originally taken up, it was now decided to concentrate all the troops available for the purpose within the inner line of works.

The losses of the English cavalry on this day amounted to

> 13 officers and 150 men killed.
> 27 ditto   and 154 ,, wounded.
>
> ————   ———
>
> 40   304
>   381 horses killed.

Russian loss.

> 6 officers and 232 men killed.
> 20 ditto and 292 ,,   wounded.
>
> ————   ———
>
> 26   524

Although the Russians may be said to have obtained a certain amount of success in their attack of the position at Balaclava, still in the main object, the capture of the place, they were defeated. If, however, after the capture of the Turkish forts, General Liprandi, in making a forward movement with cavalry, had supported them at once with his infantry and artillery, the result might have been different.

The consequences immediately resulting from the battle of the 25th of October were, therefore, apparently of no great importance. The vicinity of the enemy gave a feeling of insecurity, and the Woronzoff road, hitherto available as a partial means of communication from Balaclava to the plateau, was so no longer. But the contingent results were of very great moment. Balaclava, our only harbour and depôt, was no longer safe. The enemy were close, and might, unseen, collect an overpowering force, and regain possession of it, in spite of the vigilance of Sir Colin Campbell and the troops under his orders. In order, as far as possible, to insure its safety, two regiments of Highlanders were added to the garrison. The position was deeply intrenched from end to end, and a battery (marked G) constructed and manned by sailors over Kadikoi. A brigade of French troops were encamped on the heights behind in support. A continuous strong line of intrenchment was also made by the French and Turks round the "col de Balaclava," and extending quite down to Kadikoi. Still, Lord Raglan felt uneasiness; for in his despatch of the 3rd of November he openly confesses, that he should be more satisfied if he could have occupied the position in considerably greater strength.

On the other hand, and to provide against the contingency of a successful attack by the enemy, and to render its loss less severe, preparations were made for an immediate evacuation, to be carried out if necessary. For this purpose drag-ropes were attached to the guns on the heights, and all ships not immediately or urgently required were ordered to leave the harbour.

It will thus be evident that the Commander-in-chief was placed between two difficulties :—

1. By leaving the ships with stores, ammunition, provisions, and forage in Balaclava, he ran the risk of their capture at any moment by the enemy.

2. By anchoring them outside they became exposed to the fury of the elements, which proved a still more dangerous alternative.

To have landed the stores would have encumbered Balaclava, and the first risk still remained. By sending the ships away to sea, their contents would not be available when wanted. At a later period, and in its proper place, this subject will be renewed.

————

The previous remarks on the prospects of the siege, to which we may now return, will have led to a conviction that the crisis could not be deferred for any length of time, and that the chief hope rested on the chance of the French gaining possession of the bastion-du-mât, either by sap or assault.

We must, however, go back for a few days to notice a circumstance which had occurred at Inkermann. The enemy had erected a battery on their heights, overlooking the valley of the Chernaya, and close to the ruins of Inkermann, from which, at long range across the valley, they occasionally shelled the camp of the second division. In order to check this annoyance, a small battery called, indifferently, "the Sand-bag," or "the two-gun" battery, was erected on the 20th October, in advance of our right, and on the edge of the slope, also overlooking the Chernaya. In this were placed two 18-Pr. guns, which for a day or two opened against the enemy without much result, and were then withdrawn.

The circumstance is in itself of no great importance, but this small battery became afterwards so celebrated, as having been the scene of the heroic defence by the Guards, on the 5th of November, that its position and the purpose for which it was erected are of interest, more particularly as the fact of its having no parapet for musketry has been insisted upon as neglect; whereas its construction was for a specific purpose, and bore no reference to the defence of the heights, for which, indeed, its position was not particularly well calculated. The contest for its possession on the day of Inkermann was consequently a mere accidental circumstance.

SORTIE OF 26TH OCTOBER.

On the afternoon of the day following the battle of Balaclava, the Russians again attacked our position; choosing on this occasion the ground at Inkermann in front of the 2nd division.

This movement is generally considered to have been a reconnaissance in force, with the view of ascertaining the exact position of our troops, and whether any works of defence existed there; and it was, in fact, the shadow of a coming event.

The supposition that this point had been weakened by the withdrawal of troops to reinforce Balaclava probably influenced the Russians in their choice of the day. Their columns (variously estimated at from 6000 to 10,000 men) with artillery, and covered with skirmishers, advanced with much confidence, but were received by the 2nd division, who were formed with two batteries in advance of their own camp. The right of the line was also at once supported by H. R. H. the Duke of Cambridge, with the brigade of guards and one battery. General Bosquet also moved up with some French troops.

In half an hour the enemy's artillery abandoned the field, and their whole force retreated, and were chased down the ridges towards the head of the bay.

8

CASUALTIES ON THE 26TH OF OCTOBER.

English   Killed and wounded 80

Russians
{ Killed 130
  Prisoners 80
  Total loss supposed to be about 600

The journal of the siege for the next few days contains no very remarkable incident. The French persevered in pushing on their trenches towards the bastion-du-mât. Lord Raglan's despatch of the 3rd of November says—" That there is no material diminution of the enemy's fire; that the French have taken advantage of more favourable ground, and are carrying on approaches systematically on the most salient and commanding part of the enemy's lines, but have not succeeded in silencing their guns." Canrobert, on the 2nd of November, writes to the effect, that the operations proceed slowly but surely, and that his trenches are within 140 metres of the place; that his fire is superior, but the enemy repair their works.

The time, however, had now fully arrived when it was imperatively necessary that no further delay should occur in coming to a decision as to the adoption of final measures. The French trenches were close to the place; their army had been considerably reinforced, and there was still sufficient ammunition remaining for a short and heavy cannonade.

Consequently, at a council of war, which assembled on Saturday, the 4th, a general assault was decided upon for the 7th of November. But the enemy, anticipating our plans, and having received immense reinforcements, made another terrific attempt to raise the siege, and on the morning of the 5th of November fought a battle, which, although unsuccessful in its great object of driving the allies into the sea, still caused a great change in the views of the allied commanders; entirely postponed any idea of assault; gave time for completing the defences of Sebastopol, and thus enabled the city to hold out for ten months longer.

CHAPTER XI.

BATTLE OF INKERMANN.

ONE of the points among the many that have been urged against Lord Raglan, is his alleged neglect in not intrenching the extreme right of his position at Inkermann. Now in discussing a point of this kind, it should be considered as a part of the general question, and not as an isolated fact. It has already been explained that from deficiency of numbers it was found impossible to complete the investment up to the head of the harbour, and that, therefore, this part of the position doubtless was weak. But the troops employed in the trenches before Sebastopol were already overworked, and were diminishing from sickness and wounds at the rate of about 100 a day. It has been shown also that the safety of Balaclava hung upon a thread, and Lord Raglan in a public despatch states his inability to reinforce it. In fact, we were too weak in numbers everywhere. The regiments of the 2nd division under Sir de Lacy Evans were at Inkermann, but even they could not be altogether spared for its defence, but took a certain share in the trench duties. The number of effective men in this division, previous to the battle, amounted to about 2800, and from official returns it appears, that 1400, or one half, were away from camp on duty, night and day. Sir de Lacy Evans, who was aware of the danger of attack there, and had pointed it out both to Lord Raglan and General Canrobert, in a letter written afterwards gives what was doubtless the real cause of its not having been intrenched. He says,—" The various exigencies to be provided for on other points at that time scarcely left it possible, I believe, to afford any material reinforcements or means for the construction of defences."

It would, therefore, certainly appear that this imputation against Lord Raglan was unjust, and that the cause of its not having been intrenched was one beyond his control.

It is quite true that the ground was intrenched immediately after the battle, and this has been cited as a proof that it might have been done before; but the circumstances had then assumed quite a different phase. Offensive operations had been necessarily abandoned by the allies for the time, and the question became simply one of saving themselves from being driven into the sea. Therefore more men were available, and a considerable portion of General Bosquet's troops assisted in the construction of forts there, and also subsequently in front of the light division.

There is no doubt that, up to the time of Inkermann,

by far the greater share of the toils and dangers of the
campaign had fallen to the lot of the English.   They
had the brunt at Alma, at Balaclava, and also at
Inkermann.   This had also been made a matter of
accusation against Lord Raglan, and he has been
supposed thus to have been outwitted by his ally.   A
curious argument certainly to employ; because
supposing that the French general did nurse his own
troops at the expense of the English, and thus, by
leaving the latter more ground to occupy than they
could properly defend, led to such a battle as Inkermann, it was not a proof, by any means, of the French
general's skill, but was a great military blunder on
his part.   Sufficient is not yet known of these matters
to form a just conclusion, but there is good reason
even now for supposing that Lord Raglan in this
respect, as in others, was not the careless, incapable
general which was so commonly represented at the
time; and the more light that is thrown upon the
remarkable events of that war, the more brightly will
his character stand out, as a soldier and an English-
man.

To revert to Inkermann.   With regard to the
ground itself on which the battle was fought, except
that the numbers to defend it were so few, it offered
no very inviting facilities to any enemy's attack.   It
was a corner of the plateau, elevated several hundred
feet above the valley of the Chernaya and the marsh
at the head of the harbour.   The ascent on these sides
was very steep and difficult even for infantry, and in

some places it was quite perpendicular.   There were but two roads leading up to it, one from Sebastopol, crossing the Careening Bay ravine; the other from the north side by a narrow causeway across the marsh, and then winding up the heights.

The ground, therefore, was difficult for an attacking force, as even when it had gained the crest of the plateau, the space was restricted by steep slopes on one side and by the Careening Bay ravine on the other, so that the enemy's columns had no room to deploy.   It was undoubtedly partly owing to the confined nature of the ground that the English, only 8000 strong, were enabled for several hours to resist the attack of a vastly superior force, computed at nearly 60,000 men.

The Russians at the beginning of November received large reinforcements, two divisions of General Dannenberg's corps having been conveyed from the interior by rapid marches, in the light carriages of the country, in addition to the division of General Liprandi which had arrived in October.   Prince Menschikoff having received these reinforcements, and finding that his attack on Balaclava (although partially successful) had not obliged the allies to relinquish their offensive operations against Sebastopol, and feeling that at any hour they might successfully assault the place, determined to make another decisive attempt to avert so great a catastrophe, and, if possible, to drive the allies altogether from their position.   The plan was a bold one, although it did not altogether succeed, and was ably arranged in its details, although they also partially failed in execution. It is remarkable how exactly it was timed so as to anticipate the dreaded assault.

The general plan was as follows :—Two corps of the Russian army under General Dannenberg were detailed for the grand attack at Inkermann. The one under General Pauloff to march from the north side, and, crossing the marsh by the causeway, was then to wind up the heights in front of the 2nd division, and force the English right. Simultaneously with General Pauloff's movement, the other corps under General Soimonoff was to leave Sebastopol by a road near the Malakoff, and then march up the heights in its front, having its *left* touching the *left* side of the Careening Bay ravine, which would thus have brought it up in front of the English light division. These arrangements seem simple enough, and it is, therefore, singular that an error, apparently insignificant in itself, should have frustrated them in execution, and should have been one cause of the defeat of the Russians on the day of the battle. It appears that General Soimonoff, looking from Sebastopol, imagined that the side of the Careening Bay ravine which he was ordered to take was the left side, as he saw it from that point of view, whereas, in reality, the intention was precisely the reverse.

The result was that on the morning of the 5th of November, Soimonoff led his corps across the ravine, and up on the proper *right* hand side, and thus found himself on the ground in front of the English 2nd division, so that when General Pauloff's leading regiments arrived, the ground intended for their attack was already occupied, and the battle had begun. This error was a most unfortunate one for the Russians, as the ground was already very confined, and their columns and artillery, therefore, encumbered each other throughout the day, and could not find sufficient room to deploy.

It was also Prince Menschikoff's intention that the columns of Generals Soimonoff and Pauloff, on reaching the English position, should be united under the command of General Dannenberg, and whilst the latter was occupied in driving the allies before him, the Russian reserves should at once commence intrenching themselves on the ground at Shell Hill.* It is related in a Russian account that gabions and fascines were carried up for that purpose, and Prince Menschikoff in his despatch states, that owing to his retreat he was unable to complete the redoubts he had commenced. Had he succeeded in holding the ground sufficiently long to carry out this part of his project, the condition of the allies would have been critical; their batteries before the city would have been taken in reverse, and therefore have been untenable, and it is difficult to perceive what line of defence they could have taken up with any safety.

In order, if possible, to insure the success of his

* The ground in front of the second division was called "Shell Hill."

great scheme, and to distract the attention of the allies, Prince Menschikoff ordered several simultaneous diversions to be made. One from Sebastopol on the extreme left of the French trenches; another at Bala-clava; and a third by General Gortschakoff in front of Bosquet's position, so as to prevent the latter from assisting at Inkermann. There was also to be a general cannonade from the Russian batteries in the town.

As regards the arrangements of the English at Inkermann previous to the battle, it appears that about 500 men of the 2nd division with three field guns were detailed daily for piquets in advance of their camp, over the ground on which the battle was after-wards fought; the main piquet being at a barrier on the road where it led down the ridge to the valley. One or two slight earthworks also had been thrown up on the rising ground in front of the 2nd division. There was also a piquet of the light division at some distance down the Careening Bay ravine, the men composing which were taken prisoners on the morning of the battle.

The night of the 4th was dark, wet, and foggy. The noise of wheels is stated to have been heard during the night by the piquets of the light division; but it is curious that even up to half past 5 a.m. on the 5th the piquets of the 2nd division reported all quiet in their front.

In describing the battle of Inkermann, it is impos-sible to give accurately the positions of the various corps and batteries who took part in it, because in the first place the piquets of the 2nd division, with whom it commenced, were composed of different regiments, and, as they were driven back, they were supported by parts of their own and of others who had been hurriedly turned out; these, in turn, were reinforced by the Guards, and by regiments of the light division on their right and left, and subsequently by the 4th division as it came up to the ground. Many of the regiments also were very weak in numbers, having companies absent at the time on other duty; all were heavily engaged from the moment they arrived; besides which the ground was so overgrown with brushwood that it was difficult to preserve their formation. The plan of the battle is, therefore, only intended to indicate roughly the position of the regiments, as also those of the enemy.

It was dark and wet, and a thick fog lay on the ground, as the day dawned on the 5th of November, and the English piquets were suddenly alarmed by the approach of the Russian advanced skirmishers. A Russian account thus describes it :*—" It was on the one hand the advanced guard of Soimonoff's column advancing from Sebastopol ; on the other hand it was the two regiments of rifles from Pauloff's column approaching with their sharpshooters in advance, and

---

* This so called Russian account is faulty in many respects as to the English movements, but it appears to be reliable as regards those of the enemy, and therefore several quotations have been made from it.

beginning to climb the precipitous heights from the Inkermann side. The fog and their grey coats kept them invisible till they were close at hand. The piquets of the 2nd English division on the extreme right wing had only just distinguished through the drizzling rain the Russian riflemen climbing up, when they were compelled by the whistling of their bullets to retire to the crest of the hill, defending, however, every yard as they went. Immediately afterwards the piquets of the light division found themselves attacked from the town side, and compelled to retire.

" The English now supposed they had to do with a sortie on a large scale ; but what puzzled and confused them entirely was, that not only on the left, and in the front, there was a heavy fire of artillery ; but that also in the rear towards Balaclava there were heard volleys of artillery and musketry. It was Gortschakoff's effecting their diversion against the Sapoune (Bosquet's) heights." * * * *

The English piquets, although surprised, behaved with great gallantry, and by disputing the ground gave time to our troops to get under arms. One detachment in falling back held the Sand-bag battery for a short time, but were driven out by the enemy. The 2nd division, commanded by General Pennefather, with two batteries, was at once formed on the ridge in front of their own camp, and part of the 41st and 49th regiments were pushed forward on the right to the Sand-bag battery, and were supported there by three guns from the first division. In the mean time, the other divisions of the English army got under arms and hastened to the front, the three regiments of Guards proceeding to the right, and General Buller's brigade to the left, of the 2nd division. General Codrington's brigade took up the ground in front of its own camp on the left side of the Careening Bay ravine, being the very spot where it had been intended that Soimonoff's corps should have deployed. The latter general, however, without waiting for Pauloff's corps, was now heavily engaged in front of the 2nd division.   His artillery, which on gaining the crest of the plateau had formed line, was in action, and opened fire at a range of about 1200 yards, and Soimonoff then advanced his columns to the attack.

The Russian account, after alluding to their General's mistake, thus proceeds :—" The disadvantage of this false direction was, that from the confined nature of the ground, his (Soimonoff's) troops were very much in the way of Pauloff's column, and neither the one nor the other could find space to deploy.   Everywhere, as they were compelled to move in columns, they suffered extremely during the long way they had to march, from the severe fire of their antagonists.

" While the Russians were moving about in columns of companies, the English were drawn up in a line two deep, and their long ranging guns enabled them to inflict mortal wounds on the Russians at a time when the latter were unable to reach them at all with their fire-arms.   Nevertheless, thanks to the courage, and to the unshakeable steadiness of the Russian soldiery, the action wore at the commencement a favourable aspect, not so much in consequence of their numerical superiority, as on account of the unexpectedness of the attack, and the surprise in the fog, which, by magnifying every object in its dim obscurity, showed the English large masses everywhere."

It goes on to state that this first attack was made with 20 battalions.

Whilst the Russian columns were thus pressing forward, and threatening by the mere weight of their numbers to break through the thin English line, it is necessary to give some detailed account of the manner in which they were met. On the right the enemy had again possessed themselves of the Sand-bag battery. The Guards, however, now arrived, led by H. R. H. the Duke of Cambridge. The Grenadiers, followed by the Fusiliers (each regiment only about 400 strong), at once advanced, charged the enemy, and drove them out of the battery. Finding themselves isolated, and 700 yards in advance of the main line, the Guards not only occupied the battery, but threw out their right to cover that flank, and extended back their left towards the 2nd division, but did not reach it. The Coldstreams (about 500 strong) arrived soon to their support. In this prominent position the Guards continued to maintain themselves, in spite of the most furious attacks on both flanks.

It was about 7 o'clock a.m. when Lord Raglan and his staff arrived on the ground, and in time to witness their advance; he posted himself on the right flank, and in rear of the battery. He had previously to his arrival sent orders to Sir George Brown and Sir George Cathcart to support the 2nd division; and to Sir Richard England, who commanded the 3rd division, to guard the trenches, and prevent the enemy forcing themselves up the intermediate ravines. He had also sent officers to Generals Canrobert and Bosquet, asking for instant reinforcements.

The Russian account of the advance of the English Guards is as follows :—" The battle raged forwards, backwards, beneath, above, among bushes and under-wood ; above all, the redoubt (Sand-bag battery) on the wing had been the object of many an attack, until at length General Bentinck led up his Guards, the *élite* of the English army. These chosen troops pressed irresistibly forward to the redoubt, tore it from the Russians, and consigned it to the safe keeping of the Coldstreams. Thus ended the first act of the bloody drama, which was soon followed by one still more sanguinary. In spite of the resolute attacks of the Russians, the English had given another proof of their military virtues, and had made an heroic defence." * *

Whilst the battle was thus raging on the right, the English were equally hard pressed in the centre and on the other flank of their line. The 88th, in advancing on the left along the edge looking into the Careening Bay ravine, were surrounded, but were relieved by a charge of the 77th. In the centre, the enemy's columns were so close that the batteries there frequently fired case into them.

The Russian account says :—" The conflict commenced almost simultaneously along the whole line of battle, enveloped as it was in the fog, and as the Russian soldiery gave themselves little time for firing, but rather in the proud consciousness of their valour sought to reach their enemy as soon as possible with cold steel, it soon came to the most embittered engagement. With astonishment did the English see these attacks with the bayonet; they had flattered themselves with the delusion that no troops in the world could compete with their powerful well-fed men; and here did the Russians, whom they looked down on so superciliously, venture to challenge them to it, to attack them, and what is more, to put them to the rout; for the Russians' favourite weapon ever since Suwarrow's time has been the bayonet. * * * *

" The Russian artillery, however, 22 12-pounders and 16 6-pounders belonging to Soimonoff's column, did the English great damage. * * * *

" The English again rallied all their powers, and obstinately defended every inch of their encampment. In this the light troops of Brown's division, all practised shots, armed with capital Minié rifles, did good service, by picking down the Russian generals and other officers, and also the artillerymen and horses. It was thus that the action was brought to an equipoise, and it soon took a turn to our disadvantage, for the most distinguished leaders had already fallen; not only the three colonels of the three foremost regiments, even the commanders of the battalions, and a

great part of their officers were put *hors-de-combat*
by death or wounds.   Among these were the Commander of the artillery, Colonel Lajoskin, Brigadier
General Villebois, and General Soïmonoff.   Deprived
of all their superior leaders, and thus become uncertain
and wavering, the combatants gradually gave way,
and as the English, hereby inspirited, made all the
more furious attack, they fell back into the upper portion of the ravine." * * * *

This first grand attack had been made chiefly by
the troops of General Soimonoff.   After his death
they fell a good deal into confusion, and many left the
field, but the battle was renewed by the columns
under Pauloff, who, with their artillery, had arrived upon
the ground.   General Dannenberg was now in chief
command ; and Prince Menschikoff, with two Russian
Grand Dukes, were also present on the field of battle.

In the mean while, however, it is necessary to go
back a little in point of time, and to describe the
movements of the 4th English division.   Sir George
Cathcart, whose camp was not quite so near the scene
of action as the others, as soon as he heard the firing
had got his division under arms.   Several hundred of
his men, however, were in the trenches, and many of
them had only just returned from that duty.   Leaving
the latter, with a few companies also of the 68th and
46th regiments, in camp, under the command of Brigadier Torrens, the General himself, with a weak
brigade composed of parts of several regiments and
one field battery, proceeded to the battle.   On arriv-

ing near the scene, as each moment gave stronger evidence of the severe nature of the struggle, Sir George sent back an aide-de-camp with orders to General Torrens to follow him with the troops which had been in the first instance ordered to remain in camp.

Sir George Cathcart conceiving the extreme right to be the point most open to danger, and having been informed by a French aide-de-camp of General Bosquet, that the enemy were trying to force it, was marching in that direction, when he was met by two staff officers, who urgently requested assistance in the centre and on the left of the line. He accordingly detached the chief part of the brigade with him, as well as the battery, towards those points, retaining one wing of the 20th, with which he still proceeded to the right, and reinforced the Guards, again sending back to General Torrens to join him there at once with the other brigade. The latter general, hurrying to the field, also received an urgent requisition for assistance in front. The enemy were still forcing the line at various points; the battery of the 4th division (just spoken of) had hardly been in action and fired a few rounds of case, than it was run into, and three of its guns were spiked, the officer commanding being killed; three guns of the 2nd division in the centre of the line were also taken for a moment by the Russians, and some of the gunners bayonetted, but in both instances the guns were retaken by the English immediately afterwards.

General Torrens therefore detached the 63rd to reinforce the left, and with the few troops remaining, being some companies of the 46th and 68th (in all not 400 men), proceeded as ordered to the extreme right. Sir George Cathcart, who was waiting there, and who was probably unaware, as every one else was at the time, of the immense superiority of the enemy in numbers at all points, was anxious to act upon the flank of the Russian troops which were storming against the Sand-bag battery. Advancing accordingly for this purpose, with the companies brought by General Torrens, as also with a few men of the Guards and of other regiments, he moved along the side of the steep slopes which led down to the valley of the Chernaya. He had not gone far when he found the enemy in his front, and also below him on his right flank, and again above on his left.

It was unfortunately at this moment that this brave distinguished general fell, shot through the head, and several officers of his staff were killed with him. General Torrens was also severely wounded. The men, almost surrounded, were withdrawn from their advanced position, but continued with other troops to maintain the ground on the flank of the battery.

It is necessary now to revert to Lord Raglan, who had remained for some time on this flank. In order to reinforce the batteries of artillery which were so heavily engaged, he had, soon after his arrival on the ground, ordered up two 18-pounder guns, which were in park at the siege depôt, near the camp of the light

9 *

division; and these with the field guns were so admirably served throughout the day, that Prince Menschikoff, in his despatch afterwards, partly attributes his defeat to the fact of the English having placed their siege artillery in position. The two 18-pounder guns had no less than seventeen casualties among the men who served them, and they, as well as the batteries of the 2nd division, fired away upwards of 80 rounds of ammunition per gun during the day; a very large proportion for one action.

Lord Raglan, anxious if possible to gain some commanding point which would enable him in any partial drifting of the mist to obtain a more definite notion of the disposition and numbers of the enemy, was moving with his staff along the ridge in front of the 2nd division camp, when a shell suddenly burst among them, bringing several officers and their horses to the ground. General Strangways, who was in command of the Royal Artillery, and who at the moment was riding at Lord Raglan's side, was one of those struck by it, and was lifted off his horse and laid upon the ground by General Estcourt the Adjutant-General of the army. His left leg had been shattered by the blow. After a short delay he was carried to the camp of the siege train; but the shock was so great that he gradually sank, and died in about an hour afterwards. His death was a great loss to the army, and a terrible blow to the officers and men of his own corps. As an artilleryman he had achieved distinction years before, both at the battles of Leipsic and at Waterloo. In his life he had always been beloved, and in his death was deeply regretted.

The battle had lasted several hours. All the available regiments of the English divisions were engaged, and they had already suffered the most fearful losses. Eight of their generals had been killed * or wounded, and many other officers of rank and a large proportion of the men had fallen. Their line had already been forced several times, although in each case the enemy had been unable to retain the ground. The Russian columns still, however, persisted in their attacks. The English ammunition was failing everywhere, and at length the Guards, who for hours had held the Sand-bag battery against overwhelming odds, were driven back and formed up in line, with parts of several regiments in front of the 2nd division camp. It was a critical moment, and is thus described in the Russian account :—

* The following are the names of general officers killed and wounded at Inkermann:

Killed Generals.	Cathcart,	Commanding 4th Division.
	Strangways,	Commanding Royal Artillery.
	Goldie,	Commanding Brigade.
Wounded Generals.	Sir G. Brown,	Commanding Light Division.
	Buller,	Commanding Brigade.
	Bentinck,	Commanding Guards.
	Adams,	Commanding Brigade, died of his wounds.
	Torrens,	Commanding Brigade, died of his wounds.

"The battle had now attained its climax; it was raging among the tents on the flank and in rear of the 2nd division; most of the English generals were *hors-de-combat*. The Britons, sadly reduced in numbers, and exhausted by the length of the struggle, defended themselves but faintly. More and more the fortune of the day inclined to the Russians: they had still four regiments unemployed, while the enemy had brought up all their reserves. It was about 11 o'clock, when, on a sudden, the shrill tones of horns were heard above the rolling and rattling of the firing. The third act, the turning point of the battle, commenced. The French arrived. In the same proportion as the assurance of this timely aid revived the sinking spirits of the English, it discouraged the Russians, who felt themselves at once on the point of being deprived of the fruit of five hours hard fighting." * * * *

Again,—" In the ranks of the Russians opposed to them, General Dannenberg, who had arrived on the ground early, was distributing his orders from a rising ground near the batteries, and assigning to each column, as it came up, the point for its attack. Around him also death was busy, and struck to the ground by his side, adjutants, officers of the état-major, officers bringing reports or fetching orders. For a long time he and his beautiful brown charger remained unhurt. On a sudden his horse sank beneath him, struck by a grenade on the shoulder, and another horse was brought him by an orderly. At the moment the General was about to mount this fresh horse, another ball also laid it low, and a third was procured. Death was raging abroad, and spared neither the highest nor the lowest, but yet could not subdue the courage, the resolution, and the invincible steadiness of all." * * * *

Welcome indeed was the arrival of their gallant allies to the English on that day. Led by General Bourbaki, the regiments of the first brigade that arrived, with that dashing intrepidity for which the French are so distinguished, immediately pressed forward into the thick of the fight, and almost reached the Sand-bag battery, the contest for which had so often been renewed. But even these fresh troops found difficulty in maintaining themselves, and, as stated by General Bosquet in his despatch, were almost surrounded. A second brigade, however, quickly reinforced them, and several French batteries coming up on the right of the English ones, the enemy were at length definitely driven from the ground, and had now no alternative but a difficult retreat down precipitous slopes.

Lord Raglan's despatch, speaking of the close of the battle, says :—" Subsequently to this, the battle continued with unabated vigour and with no positive result, the enemy bringing upon our line, not only the fire of all their field batteries, but those in front of the works of the place, and the ship guns, till the afternoon, when the symptoms of

giving way first became apparent ; and shortly
after, although the fire did not cease, the retreat
became general, and heavy masses were observed
retiring over the bridge of the Chernaya, and ascending the opposite heights, abandoning on the
field of battle five or six thousand dead and
wounded, multitudes of the latter having already
been carried off by them. I never before witnessed
such a spectacle as the field presented, but upon
this I will not dwell." * * * *

The Russian account, though incorrect in some
points, is still worth quotation : — " Thus these
troops of Pauloff were now opposed to a force of
more than twice their number, after a three hours'
fight, after a night march along a sticky soil,
and after climbing steep acclivities. Victory under
these circumstances was out of the question. Their
task was now to retire with as little loss as possible of men, guns, and honour. This was indeed
difficult, posted as they were on the edge of precipitous ground, with an overpowering enemy ready
to crush them, supported by the combined English and French batteries. They had to rescue
their guns from the heights on which they were,
and bring them off along the road by which they
had come. The slightest wavering would have
seen them hurled over the steep sides of the
plateau : they gave way, therefore, gradually, and
maintained their steady retreat, step by step, and
troop by troop.

" General Dannenberg now advanced one of his two reserve regiments (Vladimir), to cover the retreat of the troops towards the town, and towards the sappers' road, into the Inkermann valley, and over the bridge into the camp on the north. The combined English and French did not venture to pursue them further than the old post road, on account partly of the resolute bearing of the Vladimir regiment, partly on account of the firing of the retiring artillery, and partly on account of the frightful ravages produced in their ranks, by the enormous shells thrown from the decks of the steamers Chersonese and Vladimir, which had, as a matter of precaution, been anchored in the bay at the mouth of the Chernaya."

" Thus ended the battle, one of the most sanguinary on record, at 2 o'clock p.m. after lasting eight hours. And what was it that foiled the Russian attack ? The bravery and stedfastness of the English ? Undoubtedly much must be laid to this account, for they were splendid, and the British soldier fought worthy of his best days. But the Russians fought no less bravely, and bravery alone did not decide it.

" Was it the superiority of the English arm ? The use of the Minié ? This weapon certainly produced great effects ; at a distance of 1500 paces, it deprived the Russian regiments of their officers ; on the other hand, the Russian sharp-shooters, only 96 to each regiment, with guns that could kill only at 1000 paces, killed and wounded as many English officers, and more generals.

" Was it the false direction that Soimonoff took ? In great measure, for the reasons already given, to which must be added that of his own death, which completed the disaster, and rendered his regiments ineffective for the remainder of the day.   Another disadvantage was that the columns, instead of arriving at their destinations simultaneously, came up one after the other.

" All these circumstances conspired to the dis-advantage of the Russian attack ; but that which was most fatal, was the incorrect execution of the sham attacks or diversions, more particularly of that one which failed to prevent Bosquet's coming to the assist-ance of the English, and it was this that decided the fortune of the day."   *   *   *   *

About 1 p.m. the fog, which had hitherto shroud-ed the movements of the Russians, partially cleared, and they were then found to be retiring.   When Lord Raglan perceived that the enemy were giving ground and retreating ; when he saw their artillery disappearing from the plateau, knowing the pre-cipitous nature of the slopes they had to descend in all the confusion of defeat, and the narrow causeway they had to cross to reach the north side, he felt at once the importance of an immediate pursuit.   His own regiments were too exhausted, and had suffered too heavily, to permit of their advancing ; but there were several thousand French troops in reserve, who had not been in action. Consequently he urged on the French general to follow up the enemy with his fresh infantry and artillery, pointing out that the result would be almost the annihilation of the Russian army. But General Canrobert hesitated until too late, and allowed the enemy to make good their retreat. It was always a matter of regret to Lord Raglan, that the exhaustion of, and terrible loss which had been sustained by, his army, thus deprived him of the power to follow up the victory.

The arguments used in French accounts of the battle, that the fire from the steamers and from the works of the place prevented their troops following up the Russians on this occasion, are hardly satisfactory when it is considered what a great result was at stake. The guns of the steamers were firing at too great an elevation, and those of the works were too distant, to be very effective.

Towards sunset two French battalions and a battery moved forward to the edge of the ridge, and from that point the allied commanders watched the Russian columns streaming across the causeway, and up the opposite slopes. Lord Raglan afterwards stated his opinion that he must have been attacked by at least 50,000 men.

The enemy, with their usual care, succeeded in carrying off all their guns, although many of them must have been disabled. A few carriages and five ammunition waggons were, however, left on the field; and remains of others which had been exploded in the retreat were found months afterwards, lying about the slopes that lead to the Chernaya.

There is probably no record of any battle in which such great numbers fought on so small a space as that of Inkermann. There are few which have been so stoutly contested, or in which the valour and perseverance of all the troops engaged have been throughout so conspicuous. The conduct of the English infantry is immortal. Although enfeebled by previous fatigue and constant night watches; still on the day of trial for hours did 8000 men resolutely maintain themselves, against successive columns of attack of vastly superior numbers; and at last, when almost overpowered, they found an ever ready and gallant ally at hand to save them in their hour of need.

It was a battle also which brought conspicuously forward the sterling courage and unmatched steadiness of the English artillery. The Russian columns repeatedly were close to the muzzles of their guns, and were driven back by volleys of case. In some instances, the batteries were actually run into, and the gunners bayonetted at their posts. Both Lord Raglan's and Menschikoff's despatches bear tribute to the effect they produced by their fire. The casualties in the English batteries amounted to 96 men. Their carriages were repeatedly struck, and they had 80 horses killed.

The fact of the Russians having brought to the field heavier guns than those of the English, has been assumed as a proof of their general superiority in this

branch of the service; but without detracting from
their merits, it is evident that although for the purposes of a single battle, close to their own arsenal,
they might venture to bring out ordnance of a heavy
calibre, it does·not follow that these would be available, or adapted for the ordinary purposes of a campaign.

The undoubted bravery of the Russian army was
sullied by their atrocious conduct to the wounded
English, who for a moment during some of the attacks
remained in their power. Their barbarity in
bayonetting them when lying helpless on the ground,
is only equalled by their perfect indifference to the
fate of their own wounded. Although many hundreds
had been left upon the field, they asked for no flag of
truce, and made no inquiries, so that a year and a
half afterwards, when peace was made, skeletons of
their men were found scattered about in the ravines,
many of whom had probably crept so far when
wounded, and had, thus neglected, been allowed to
die. War, always horrible in its details, is rendered
infinitely more so by such wanton barbarity.

Some writers, not exactly acquainted with the disposition and casualties of the English army during
the campaign, and knowing that 25,000 infantry had
originally landed in the Crimea, are unable to understand how it happened that only 8000 could be
made available for the defence of Inkermann on the
day of the battle. The following rough calculation
will, therefore, sufficiently explain the circumstances.

English infantry originally landed in Crimea 25,000

Losses in action, at Alma, Balaclava, and the trenches	.. 3000	
Left the army sick	5000	
Deduct troops at Balaclava, say	3000	17,000
Deduct 3rd division, of which only a small portion were engaged in the action ..	3000	
Absent in the trenches and other duties .. 3000		

Total numbers actually present about ..   8,000

The 8000 men actually present may be subdivided as follows :—

Guards	1300
Second division	2500
Light division	2000
Fourth division	2200

8000

The casualties of the English army at the battle amounted to

	Killed.	Wounded.	Missing.	Total.
Officers ..	43	101	1 ..	145
Men ..	416	1832	197 ..	2445

2590

The French had about 6000 men engaged, and their casualties amounted to about 900.

The Russian force has been calculated as follows :—

	Men.	Guns.
Soimonoff ..	25,000 ..	38
Pauloff	22,000 ..	40
	47,000 ..	78

Casualties .. 15,000

During the height of the battle (about 9 a.m.) and in pursuance of their great scheme, the Russians made a sortie against the extreme left of the French siege works. Their column was about 5000 strong, and accompanied by artillery. In the mist, they succeeded in getting into two batteries, spiked the guns, and drove out the French, who, however, rallied on receiving reinforcements, and chased the enemy back to their own works. The French, too eager in the pursuit, followed close up to the walls, where they suffered severely from the heavy fire; their gallant General De Lourmel being killed. It is supposed that the Russians lost about 1000 men in this attempt. The casualties of the French in this attack were about 800.

———————

Whatever hopes or expectations might have been previously entertained as to the speedy fall of Sebastopol, the battle of Inkermann at all events utterly and rudely dispelled them. The facts were now plain and distinct enough. Nearly 100,000 Russians were on the spot ready to defend their city to the last, and the allied armies were not much more than half the number. The Russians had already proved from the opening of the bombardment that their resources in guns, material, and ammunition, were far superior to the limited means of the allies. The latter had now pretty well exhausted their original supply. Their guns and carriages were nearly worn out, and of their ammunition only a small portion remained unexpended. The fortresses in the Mediterranean might, it is true, afford some assistance to the English in re-

plenishing their batteries, but there was no hope of
efficient offensive operations being renewed until
fresh armaments could arrive from France and England. Months must thus elapse, during which the
enemy would have time to complete their defences, to
construct inner ones, to deepen their ditches and add
to their batteries; and having also free communications with the interior, they could obtain all other
necessary supplies, and, therefore, might hope to meet
their foes again on equal terms, when the latter
should feel inclined to renew the contest.

Thus the first attempt upon Sebastopol had utterly
failed.

But even these were by no means the worst features
of the case. The allies, with open trenches and
batteries close to Sebastopol, were holding an offensive
position from which it was impossible to withdraw, at
the same time that, surrounded by superior numbers
of the enemy, who had already attacked them twice,
they had to watch carefully, lest they should be forced
at some weak point on the flank. With numbers
scarcely sufficient to maintain the defensive at one
point, it was still necessary to assume a bold attitude
of offence at the other. A truly embarrassing and
anomalous position.

But we must go farther, before we can fully realize
the difficulties which encompassed the English troops.
Not having foreseen the possibility of a winter campaign, the government had made no provision whatever
to meet the inevitable hardships it must bring with it.

The voice of the nation had called upon them to go to the Crimea, and they went. The step once taken admitted of no withdrawal; no retreat, no change of plan or of position, could now be made, either with safety or with honour. Winter was upon them, and standing on the bare plateau, with diminished numbers, without proper shelter, food, or clothing, they must now be prepared night and day, for months, to maintain their dangerous position.

It will be necessary shortly to enter into details of these matters, and to endeavour, in stating the consequences which ensued, to trace the latter to their true causes.

At this moment of almost unparalleled difficulty, when danger was present, and future trials were inevitable; in the midst of conflicting counsels and irresolute resolves, the calm attitude and undaunted courage of Lord Raglan gave confidence to others, and at the same time proclaimed the greatness and inherent superiority of his character.

It is so important to understand clearly the state of affairs at this critical turning point of the great struggle, that a short recapitulation will be interesting, in order to a full appreciation of Lord Raglan's position at the same time. Eight of his generals had fallen. Upwards of 2500 men were lying on the field of battle. The hospitals were already full. Cholera still lingered in his camp; and England had next to no reserves to recruit the ranks of the army. Winter had arrived, and the men had neither proper shelter,

10

clothes, or means of transport to bring them food. There was positively nothing obtainable in the country. The attempt on Sebastopol had failed, the siege train was exhausted, and there was no other within some thousand miles.

Lord Raglan knew all these things, and though feeling deeply the great losses he had sustained in battle, and foreseeing the great trials which were coming, he still never wavered or doubted of ultimate success. But he did not know, and he did not foresee, that still greater trials awaited him, and that at the very time his energies were given to meet and over-come these great difficulties, the English nation, misled by the press, would withdraw from him their confi-dence, and would impute to his incapacity the sad consequences which arose from previous want of pre-paration, and from other circumstances over which he had no control.

Lord Raglan did not live long enough to receive an acquittal at the hands of his country of the numerous charges brought against him; but he left a name that demands justice, and he left also a principle as a guide to the English soldier, that however difficult or pain-ful his position may be, one feeling alone should guide him, and that is, duty. He had learnt this years before in another scene, and he carried out the prin-ciple until he died. Let us hope that a man of so great and pure a character may always be found in England's hour of danger to command her army in the field.

CHAPTER XII.

On the 6th November the allied generals again met in council, to decide upon their plans for the future, which had been so materially influenced by the battle of the previous day. The idea of assault was abandoned, and it was determined at once to intrench Inkermann, and to act almost entirely upon the defensive, until the arrival of reinforcements of every kind from France and England should enable them to resume their attack upon Sebastopol.

At this period, when the hardships of the winter were just commencing, the condition of the English army, in point of numbers, began to be most alarming. Though the campaign had not lasted two months, the infantry, which at landing had amounted to 25,000, now scarcely exceeded 14,000 men, effective for duty. Death, wounds, and sickness had already diminished it in this fearful manner. The English nation, sud-

10 *

denly roused to the realities of war, was terrified at
the threatened extinction of its army.

The Times newspaper, alluding to the smallness
of the numbers available for the work they were called
upon to perform, said, that the proportions of warfare
were no longer maintained ; viz.—The besiegers to the
besieged ; the gunners to the guns ; the men in camp
to the men in trenches ; hours of rest to hours of
work ; and that such a violation of laws was sure to
avenge itself.

Day after day, the Government was urged to send
out instant reinforcements. But warnings were now
too late, and these urgent appeals could only be met
partially, and by slow degrees. There were few troops
in England to send, and even these were young and
unfit for the hardships of a campaign.

The following extract from the Report of the Committee of the House of Commons, on the " State of the
Army before Sebastopol," is clear enough on the
point :—

" The men sent out to reinforce the army were
recruits who had not yet become fit for foreign service,
and the depôts at home were too weak to feed the
companies abroad. The order to attack Sebastopol
was sent to Lord Raglan on the 29th of June. The
formation of a reserve at Malta was not determined
upon until early in November. It will be seen from
the correspondence between Lord John Russell and
Lord Aberdeen, that Lord Raglan had reported that
he wished he had been able to place in the position of

Balaclava, on the 26th of October, a more considerable force; and also that, on the 5th of November, the heights of Inkermann were defended by no more than 8000 British infantry. When the Duke of Newcastle acquainted Lord Raglan that he had 2000 recruits to send him, he replied, that those last sent were so young and unformed, that they fell victims to disease, and were swept away like flies; he preferred to wait.

" In December, the power of reinforcing the army with efficient soldiers was so reduced that the Government thought it necessary to introduce a foreign enlistment bill, for the purpose of raising a foreign legion.

" Your committee must express their regret that the formation of a large reserve at home, and also in the proximity of the seat of war, was not considered at a much earlier period; and that the Government, well knowing the limited numbers of the British army, the nature of the climate in the East, as well as the power we were about to encounter, did not, at the commencement of the war, take means to augment the ranks of the army beyond the ordinary recruiting; and also that earlier steps were not taken to render the militia available both for the purpose of obtaining supplies of men, and also, in case of necessity, for the relief of regiments of the line stationed in garrisons in the Mediterranean—measures which they found themselves compelled to adopt at a later period." * * * *

As a contrast to our feebleness at this time, the Emperor Napoleon was able to inform France that his army amounted to 581,000 men, and 113,000 horses. With this enormous reserve, the French army in the Crimea could be rapidly augmented to almost any amount; at the same time, care was taken that not only men were sent, but large waggon trains and establishments accompanied them, so that every branch increased in proportion, and the troops were at once available for the siege operations.

It was in this respect that the arrangements of the French should have been taken as our guide; but with us the establishments did not exist, and consequently, even when English regiments afterwards arrived (withdrawn from the garrisons of the Mediterranean), although they added to the numerical strength on paper, in reality they only increased our difficulties; by throwing a heavier burden upon those administrative branches of the service, such as commissariat, transport, &c., in which the army was so deficient. So much was this the case, that in several instances Lord Raglan was obliged to encamp regiments at Balaclava on their arrival, in order to be near the depôts; though their presence with the army before Sebastopol would have been invaluable, had the means existed of moving them, and of providing for them, when sent there.

In the mean time, whilst the army was so arduously engaged in holding its position before Sebastopol, and just as it was beginning to suffer the terrible hardships of the winter of 1854, a frightful disaster at sea added greatly to the difficulties by which it was already surrounded. It has been shown that the contingent results of the battle of Balaclava were to render the harbour unsafe in a military point of view, and therefore made it necessary to leave as few ships in it as possible; at all events until the position could either be strengthened, or some other expedient be adopted. It was unfortunately during this period, and whilst the arrangements of this our only harbour were partially upset, that a gale, unprecedented in its violence, overtook the exposed fleet of transports anchored off Balaclava, Eupatoria, and the Katcha, in which many of them were sunk, containing forage and other valuable stores, the want of which afterwards added so much to the hardships and sufferings of the army.

The reason for detaining so many sailing ships on the coast in attendance on the troops was, that during the month of October and the early part of November, Lord Raglan had of necessity remained uncertain as to what might be the final disposal of his army for the winter, and as to whether it might not suddenly leave the Crimea. The greater part were horse transports, and these, by his orders for the same reason, were kept supplied with forage. Their loss consequently involved that of about 20 days' forage for the whole army.

With respect to the bay outside Balaclava, in which some of the transports were necessarily detained, it was generally supposed at the time, that the north and the north-west winds were the prevailing ones, from which this anchorage was tolerably protected.

The following is a list of the transports lost in the gale.

Place of anchorage.	Name.	Contents.
	Prince—Steamer	40,000 great coats, winter clothing, drugs, ammunition, &c. &c.
	Resolute	Reserve infantry, and field artillery ammunition, and stores.
Outside Balaclava	Kenilworth	
	Wild Wave	Horse transports, with forage on board.
	Rip-van-Winkle	
	Progress	Hay and barley.
	Wanderer	Oats.
	Peltona	Biscuit.
Off the Katcha	Pyrenees	
	Ganges	Horse transports, with forage on board.
	Rodsley	
	Tyrone	
Off Eupatoria	Her Majesty	
	Asia	Horse transports, with forage on board.
	Glendalough	

The loss of the "Prince" was occasioned by the falling overboard of her masts, which thus fouled the screw, and prevented her from getting out to sea. The "Resolute" as a magazine ship, containing several million rounds of ball-cartridge, and also large quantities of field artillery ammunition and stores, remained in Balaclava until after the battle of the 25th of October, when, for the reasons already specified, she was ordered outside: but as her contents might be required at any moment, and, in fact, were so, after the battle of Inkermann, it was not deemed advisable to allow her to put to sea.

Although, therefore, the unprecedented violence of the gale proved a terrible misfortune to the army, it does not appear that our losses were to be attributed to the neglect of those with whom rested the disposition of the transports, but rather to the fact, that we were so hardly pressed by the enemy, that not even our one small harbour was safe, as a base of operations. The misfortunes of the gale were not limited to the number of ships actually lost. Many others were much damaged, and required great repairs. Consequently, for a time, the want of sea transport was added to the deficiency by land, and the troops were thereby prevented from receiving regular supplies of fresh meat, and other essentials, by which their already great sufferings were much augmented.

The general causes of the difficulties of the English army, and of their aggravated sufferings in the winter of 1854-55 were :—

Firstly, That in ordering the army to the Crimea, the English Government had not anticipated a winter campaign with open trenches; and provision accordingly had not been made in time for it; such as shelter, supply of clothing, fuel and forage, &c., for the army.

Secondly, That the English army was in numbers unequal to the task assigned it, and there did not exist sufficient reserves to increase it, or even to maintain its original strength.

Thirdly, That few even as the numbers were, they did not possess the establishments, such as land transport, &c., to enable an army to keep the field.

The result was, that when the bombardment of October failed, and when the enemy, by their great attack at Inkermann, had rendered it necessary to postpone active operations, Lord Raglan found himself with an enfeebled army, on a bare plateau, without proper shelter, winter clothing, or fuel; several miles from his depôts, without means of transport even for food; and at the same time, that he was under the necessity of guarding extensive open trenches, before a partially besieged town.

This state of affairs cannot fairly be imputed to any want of foresight in Lord Raglan. He had undertaken the expedition with a small force at too late a season, in compliance with the orders of his Government, and with the unanimous wishes of his country, but contrary to his own opinion. He had persevered in the attempt to capture the place, until his army had been almost overwhelmed by the immense reinforcements of the Russians. Having now rendered his position, as far as possible, safe from attack, his next efforts were directed to the sheltering and clothing, &c., of his troops during the ensuing winter.

Before entering into any detailed account of the steps taken by Lord Raglan to meet these great difficulties, it is necessary to observe, that even supposing the army had been sufficient in numbers, and properly equipped, still, under the most favourable circumstances, a winter campaign must at all times be a trying one, and must inevitably entail great hardship and a certain amount of sickness on the troops engaged in it. Lord Raglan had written home to the Government in October, as soon as he perceived the probability of a protracted struggle, pointing out the great sufferings which must ensue, with troops exposed without proper shelter during the winter; and he at once also took steps on the spot to mitigate them as far as possible.

The following is a detail of some of the principal difficulties of the English army at this time, and of the steps taken by Lord Raglan, and by those under him, to meet them :—

SHELTER FOR MEN AND HORSES.—On the 8th of November, as soon as it was finally decided that the army must winter in the Crimea, General Airey, Quarter-Master-General, with a view to the erection of huts and stabling, sent to Constantinople large orders for planking; and on the same day, and others immediately following, he sent steamers to Sinope, Trebizonde, and Samsoun with the same object. This was in anticipation of, and in addition to, the huts which the Government were about to send from England.

A large quantity of materials accordingly soon arrived ; but owing to its weight, and the want of transport, it could only be removed from Balaclava and made use of by degrees.

With respect to horses, other means were also resorted to ; spare spars, sails, tarpaulins, &c., were landed, as far as they could be spared from the transports ; but the supply was limited, and this kind of covering was difficult to erect, from the heavy spars required to support it, and was only adapted for sheltered spots. A troop of Horse Artillery, however, was protected in this way in a valley near Balaclava, and also some of the transport animals.   The horses of one battery of artillery were saved, owing to their vicinity to Balaclava, and to the energy of the officers and men in cutting down the few trees in the neighbourhood for uprights, &c., so that when planks arrived, the horses were soon under cover.   As the great difficulty to be met was want of transport, not only for planking and forage, but for every description of stores, the English cavalry were moved down from the plateau and encamped close to Balaclava at the beginning of December, in order to be near the depôts.   This precaution would have been adopted at an earlier period, but the position of the cavalry being a military question to be decided by the allied commanders, the

French General's acquiescence was required, which was not accorded in the first instance.

Another cause of delay, not only in the operation of sheltering the horses, but in every operation connected with the winter difficulties, was the want of men, especially of skilled workmen.

The huts from England did not begin to arrive until the army had suffered greatly from exposure, more especially from want of hospitals in camp.   Their great weight ($2\frac{1}{2}$ tons each), was another difficulty. Lord Raglan in his despatch dated 6th of January says, that the transport of one required 180 men. The variety of their construction, which was almost as complicated as that of a Chinese puzzle, also led to confusion and delay.

WINTER CLOTHING. — The loss of the Prince steamer on the 14th of November, with 40,000 great coats, winter clothing, provisions, medical stores, &c., was a terrible disaster at such a moment.   On the 16th, Captain (now Colonel) Wetherall was sent to Constantinople with an almost unlimited order for the purchase of warm clothing, both for men and horses.   This supply shortly arrived at Balaclava, as also immense quantities from England; but the want of transport again prevented the troops from immediately receiving these articles, which their condition so imperatively required.

Colonel Tulloch, in a pamphlet lately published,*

* The Crimean Commission and the Chelsea Board, by Colonel Tulloch.

suggests, that the men should have been sent down to Balaclava and back, 14 miles through a quagmire, to carry up these stores, although at the same time he shows that out of 11,367 effective men in January, 5321 (or very nearly half) were daily detailed for other duties. Well might General Airey say, that whilst every man was already doing the work of three, Colonel Tulloch, by way of improving their condition, suggests they should have done the work of six. The army was well clothed by the middle of January.

FORAGE.—One of the most serious deficiencies of the army, during the early part of the winter, was that of forage. It is perfectly evident that the failure of a regular supply in this essential article involves inevitable disaster, and must paralyze every depart-ment. Great as were the difficulties in preserving the lives of the cavalry, artillery, and transport horses, owing to the want of shelter, and the hard work to which they were subject, any, even temporary, want of forage must naturally soon preclude or render further exertion unnecessary.

In examining into the cause of this deficiency, it will be remembered that about 20 days' forage for the army was lost in the gale of the 14th of November; a most serious amount at such a moment. It further appears, that as early as September 13th (and before the army had disembarked) Mr. Filder, the Commis-sary General, wrote to England for 2000 tons of pressed hay; but his demands did not receive prompt attention, only a very small portion arriving in November, and the whole was not completed until the following June. In the mean time, however, Mr. Filder also endeavoured to obtain supplies nearer at hand : but he was disappointed in his contracts, and the forage of the East being chiefly chopped straw, and consequently not compressible, its bulky nature rendered it impossible to transport an adequate supply to Balaclava. When it is considered that a vessel which could hold 600 tons of pressed hay would only carry 50 tons of chopped straw, it will be readily conceived how much inconvenience would be thus occasioned in a small crowded harbour.

Lord Raglan's despatch dated the 10th of February, 1855, says,—"The health of the troops continues to improve in some slight degree. They are amply supplied with warm clothing, and with provisions. Forage is our only want, and this arises chiefly from the Commissary General not receiving from England the supplies of hay upon which he has reckoned."

About 42 per cent. of the horses of the cavalry and artillery died during the winter, and even of those which survived, almost all were much injured for future service.

BALACLAVA.—Balaclava, from its limited accommodation, and the small extent of its harbour, always inadequate as the sole place of disembarkation for the supplies of an army, became still more so under the vast accumulation of materials which arrived, and were required to be landed, in the early part of the winter. Guns, shot, shell, planks, huts, clothing, forage, &c.,

articles all either bulky or weighty, poured in without intermission.   Only one small wharf existed.   The construction of others was not only a work of time, but required skilled labour, which was sought for in vain at Constantinople, and could only be spared in a small degree from the fleet.   Still less could a sufficiency of men be spared for quickly unloading vessels ; and the stores, even when landed, encumbered the small village, owing to the oft-mentioned want of transport to convey them away.

Thus the deficiencies of the army in one point reflected their weaknesses on another.   Hence delays and mistakes of detail arose, which no administrative talent could altogether prevent, and no exertions on the spot redeem.   Under such circumstances as these, it is not difficult, for those who are anxious to prove general incompetency or mismanagement, to find out cases of confusion and apparent neglect.   A skilful person, especially after the event, may readily dress up such instances, and produce them as a type of the general administration, and thus succeed in producing false impressions, which has so frequently been done as regards the misfortunes of the army in the winter of 1854.

The great size of the English transports was an additional inconvenience in so small a harbour, and their mixed cargoes added to the difficulty : especially as the shot and shell (which as being the weightiest were at the bottom,) were always wanted immediately, so that other stores, even if not urgently required, had to be landed first or displaced to get at them.

Lord Raglan, alluding to his difficulties at this period, writes on the 30th of December, 1854 :—

" We are daily receiving vast supplies of ammunition, warm clothing, and huts for the army. The utmost efforts will be made to disembark all these stores ; but the difficulty of effecting this desirable object is very great, owing to the very limited extent of the harbour, its crowded state, and the narrow entrance to the town, and want of space on the beach ; the rocks on the north side rising directly out of the water, and there being, consequently, no accommodation but on one side."

Again, on the 27th of January, 1855, he writes :— " Every exertion is making, by public transport and individually, in getting huts up ; but this is a most difficult operation, and the ground is still so rotten, that it is a most arduous labour to pass along it. The extremely confined space of Balaclava, and the vast accumulation of stores, has obliged me to erect huts at some distance outside the town for their reception.

Colonel Tulloch in his pamphlet expresses a different opinion as regards Balaclava. He says :—

" As to the difficulty of landing either of these supplies, owing to the inconveniently small size of the harbour, to which Mr. Filder in another part also alludes, it is a sufficient evidence of the futility of any

11

such objection, that the harbour was just as limited in extent at the end of the following year, when nearly thrice the number of troops, and ten times as many baggage animals, were abundantly supplied through that channel." * * * *

But there are some important omissions in Colonel Tulloch's statement, as regards the altered circum- stances in the second winter

1. As no siege was then being carried on, the vast amount of heavy guns, shot, and shell, the landing of which occupied so much time and space during the previous winter, were no longer required.

2. The army not being engaged in active opera- tions, any amount of fatigue parties could be obtain- ed for unloading vessels.

3. The existence of the railway, and of a good road, and ample transport, enabled the stores to be re- moved at once, and prevented that accumulation which was the great difficulty in the first instance.

4. Good wharves had been constructed before the second winter.

Therefore, although the harbour naturally re- mained of the same size, the facilities of landing were much greater, and the means of removing stores incomparably so.

THE ROAD FROM BALACLAVA TO THE HEIGHTS.

Among the many charges of incompetency and want of foresight brought against Lord Raglan at

the time, none, perhaps, was more strongly urged
than his alleged neglect in not making a road from
Balaclava up to the position of the army before Sebastopol.   The simple answer is, that neither men nor
means existed.   From the time of its arrival before
Sebastopol, the army was numerically inadequate to
the work required of it.   During the month of October
its ranks were diminishing at the rate of about 100 a
day, from sickness and over-work.   In the mean time
we were seriously attacked at Balaclava, almost anni-
hilated at Inkermann, and our very existence depended upon maintaining our position.   How, then, could
Lord Raglan venture to withdraw men for the purpose of road-making?

Sir de Lacy Evans, in his evidence before the House
of Commons, expressed his opinion, that " the work of
1000 men a day for 10 days would have secured the
road from Balaclava."   Such a number might have
been of some service, but could not be spared at the
time, even to intrench Inkermann.   As regards the
road, however, the experience of the next winter
proved that it required 12,000 men a day for two
months, backed up by the skilled labour of the army-
works-corps, to complete it, and with the traffic re-
ieved in the mean time by the railway.

In the report of the commissioners (Sir John
M'Neil and Colonel Tulloch), it is stated that the
" Officers commanding divisions who were examined
on the subject are unanimous in their opinion, that it
would have been impossible to employ a sufficient

11 *

number of men to make a road, and at the same time to carry on the military operations in which the army was engaged."

Colonel Tulloch (although his opinion on such a matter is entitled to little weight), in his pamphlet, and alluding to the severe duties of the army at the time, writes to the same effect; as follows :—

" 1. That such severe duties, combined with scanty nourishment and insufficient clothing, must have added greatly to the sickness and mortality.

" 2. That they necessarily precluded any such extensive undertaking, as the formation of a road to Balaclava."

Sir John Burgoyne writes :—" I would, however, observe, that it was utterly out of the question to re-duce the extent of our trenches, so as to withdraw men from that work, as has often been suggested, for the purpose of making a road. It was necessary to occupy the position. Had we narrowed our limits, the Russians would have advanced theirs, and the actual effect of our retreating from our advanced position would have been to bring the whole of our camp under cannonade. The impossibility of pausing in our process of active measures will account for many subjects of remark, in attempting what appears to have been beyond our means.

" I would submit, however, that the want of the road, which has been so much pressed, was not of the vital importance that has been represented. The want of food, that is, to the extent of the authorized ration, was very slight. The warm clothing was brought up by degrees; I admit, with much labour. All this would no doubt have been greatly alleviated by a made road; but a good supply, and a due maintenance of transport animals (without which the best road would have been useless), would have been of more value, and that essential want has arisen from defective arrangements and organization. If great fault is to be found, I think it should be attached to these defects.

"To retire to Balaclava was utterly impossible, and the other alternative of taking the field was as impossible by the British with their very small force. Turks, or other natives, for work, were proved to be unavailing. 500 Turkish soldiers (by far the best native labour at our disposal), under the guidance of engineer officers, were employed several days in attempts to improve the road, but they were found quite inefficient. They could make no impression on the deep compact clay of which the country was composed, and Lord Raglan at length ordered the work to be discontinued." * * * *

TRANSPORT.—The above able remarks of Sir John Burgoyne prove clearly the impossibility of withdrawing the men from our position at the time for the purpose of making a road, and they at the same time point out the one great deficiency and source of weakness which perpetually afflicted our army—the want of transport.

I have already frequently alluded to the total

absence of anything in the shape of transport at the commencement of the war, and, as a consequence, to our inability to advance to the Danube, even had it been desirable; to the futile attempts made to improvise a corps at Varna; to our difficulties on the march, and again in supplying our batteries with ammunition during the first bombardment. But it was reserved for the winter of 1854 to display the helplessness of an army ordered to take the field, without the means of supplying its daily wants; and to prove to what an extent an army may suffer from undertaking a task beyond its powers, and without long previous preparation and careful study.

The Commissariat transport of the army, on landing at Old Fort, consisted of about 70 mule carts. A certain number of arabas drawn by oxen or camels were seized in the neighbouring villages. Soon after our arrival at Balaclava, and from time to time, Mr. Filder received large supplies of the pack animals which had been left behind at Varna. Some hundred animals were also purchased early in the winter at Eupatoria. Hard work, inclement weather, want of shelter, and irregular supplies of forage, caused immense losses. But it will be seen that the transport of the army, such as it was, consisted rather of a miscellaneous collection than of an organized corps; and this was a radical defect.

The Times newspaper, at the period alluded to, considered that a waggon-train could be organized in a fortnight, or could be settled with contractors in ten minutes; but such remarks are loose, inconsistent, and pregnant with error.   No greater mistake can be committed, than to suppose that military arrangements thus admit of being improvised; none require more careful preparation, and the general of an army is only hampered by attaching to his forces undisciplined corps, whether for transport or any other purposes. Mere expenditure of money cannot redeem the neglect of previous preparation.

The vast accumulation of material that poured into Balaclava at the end of 1854 added to the difficulties of the situation.   The total weight of the huts alone is estimated at 3750 tons, and that of the ammunition required for the new armament was enormous.

Many persons arguing as civilians, or only partially acquainted with the critical position of our army, and aware of the fact that numbers of guns, and large quantities of shot and ammunition, were conveyed to the camp from Balaclava during the winter, are unable to conceive how, under such circumstances, any deficiency of transport really existed, or why the whole was not devoted to the actual wants of the men. But the truth is, that the replenishing of our batteries was essential to our safety.   Once committed to the attack, the option of pausing no longer remained with us.   Progress was absolutely necessary, or the enemy would have advanced, and rendered our very camp untenable.   More particularly was this the case, when it is considered that the French trenches were close to the town.   Most gallantly and indefatigably for months the French maintained themselves in this

advanced post, and it was not only necessary for the
general safety, but our bounden duty to our ally, to
support him as far as was in our power in his critical
position.   In fact, so much did this consideration
naturally press upon General Canrobert, that he was
unceasing in his inquiries as to our progress in re-
arming.   Large numbers of his men were lent to
assist in carrying up our shot and shell. His waggons
were daily employed for the same purpose; and he
once declared, that rather than further delay should
occur, every man in the French army should, if necessary, be sent to Balaclava to assist.

The Commissariat land-transport had dwindled
down, at one time, to little more than 300 animals;
and the sea-transport had been also temporarily
deranged by the gale.   Owing to this terrible state of
affairs, the troops could not receive proper food; the
clothing they so urgently required could not be
carried up from Balaclava; the huts to shelter them
remained on board ship, or encumbered the strand.
For the same reason, fuel, one of their most urgent
wants, could not be conveyed to camp.   The result
was, that the troops, suffering from over-work, exposure,
night watches, short rations, indifferent shelter, and
insufficient clothing, fell sick in such overwhelming
numbers, that in January, 1855, of the infantry before
Sebastopol,

The sick in the Crimea amounted to about 4000

The sick at Scutari and elsewhere   . .   8000

                                        Total   . .   12,000

The effective for duty at the time hardly equalled that amount.*

General Canrobert most generously afforded assistance by lending mule litters. The sick were also conveyed to Balaclava on cavalry horses, and in artillery waggons ; though both conveyances were ill adapted for the purpose.

500 cavalry horses were employed daily in December, carrying up provisions, as were also large fatigue parties of the infantry at Balaclava throughout the winter. Sleighs were also made, but the frost did not continue sufficiently long to render them available. Knowing that want of proper supervision was one cause of the casualties among the transport animals, Lord Raglan, on the arrival of 250 Spanish mules, placed them under the charge of officers and non-commissioned officers of cavalry. A cargo of buffaloes, in the same way, were, when landed, superintended and cared for by artillery-men. Thus various means were adopted to mitigate the evil.

In conclusion, the best practical proof of the importance of this branch of an army's equipment is afforded by the following detail of the land-transport corps when peace was signed.

English and native drivers	14,000
Animals	28,000
Waggons	800
Carts	1000

* The deaths in the army amounted to 9248 men in the seven winter months, not including those killed in action.

When the war began, the department was re-presented by the expressive figure—0

General Peel, in an excellent speech delivered lately in the House of Commons, thus speaks of these matters:—

" I cannot agree with the noble lord at the head of the Government, that the time of this House can be wasted by inquiries into the cause of the calamities which occurred in the Crimea (*Hear, hear*). I am aware of the ridicule to which I should naturally and justly expose myself, if I were to offer any professional opinion upon the events of the Crimean campaign; and I am aware also of the difficulties under which I labour, in speaking in the presence of so many officers who served before Sebastopol. But we may depend upon it, that the military profession is as subject to the rules of common sense, as any other (*hear*); and I see no reason why any member of this House, who has carefully examined the evidence laid on the table, should not be in a condition to form an opinion upon the question before us (*Hear*). For my own part, having passed two whole summers in investigating this matter—con-trary, I may be permitted to say, to my own wishes, and contrary to my expressed opinion as to any advantage to be derived from our inquiries —I have arrived at the opinion, that the cala-mities which occurred in the Crimea arose from circumstances which it was not in the power of any individual in the Crimea to control (*Hear,*

hear). I am happy to find that Lord Panmure expressed the same opinion in the speech which he made at Arbroath.

" The mistake of those who have been foremost in demanding inquiry into the sufferings of the Crimean army consists in the attempt to throw the blame upon individuals (*Hear, hear*). I am certain that anybody who reads the evidence given by the head of the War Department must admit that he did everything in his power to avert the calamities that befell the army, and that he was only responsible with the rest of the Government for what took place. I also believe that Admiral Boxer, Captain Christie, and Lord Raglan fell victims to that senseless clamour which was raised against them in this country upon anonymous authority (*Cheers*).

" Now, Sir, I have always attempted to remodel bad systems, instead of attacking the individuals who had to work them. Let it not for a moment be supposed, that I underrate the hardships and privations to which the army was subject, during the winter of 1854-5. So far from underrating them, I think it is impossible to exaggerate them ; and equally impossible would it be to exaggerate the patience and heroism with which they were endured (*Cheers*). But, admitting the hardships endured by this army, I believe that nobody was responsible for them. I am perfectly aware, that when I say so I may well be asked,

'What then were, in your opinion, the causes of those hardships?' I think that the time has gone by when there ought to be any delicacy whatever in answering that question. I believe that the chief cause was your commencement of a great war with little means (*Loud cries of ' Hear, hear ! '*) The army was deficient in everything but in the bravery, discipline, and boldness of its troops (*Cheers*). With that army, suffering much from sickness, you undertook a great military operation without any reserve whatever. The Government were not so responsible for that, as the country which raised the universal cry that the war should be carried on with vigour.

" I think that the Government were to blame for not having foreseen at an earlier period, the possibility of the army having to remain in the Crimea during the winter of 1854-5. I am perfectly aware that there was a general belief that the army would not have to remain there during that winter, and that it was not till after the battle of Inkermann that it became certain that it would have to winter in the Crimea. It is to the position in which the army then was, that I attribute the calamities which afterwards inevitably occurred.

" Lord Raglan had no resources whatever with which to overcome the difficulties by which he was surrounded; nor could he abandon his guns, his allies, and the honour of his country, by en-

deavouring to re-embark his army. I do not think
that he would have succeeded in that endeavour
(*Hear, hear*). But, whatever might be the severity
of the hardships which he had to endure, anybody who knew Lord Raglan must feel that he
would maintain his position as long as he had
a single regiment (*Hear, hear*).

"The army was exhausted by work beyond its
strength. It was not able to keep up that road
of communication which lay between it and the
harbour of Balaclava, where the provisions intended
for it were landed. An outcry was raised in this
country against the War Department, because that
road to Balaclava was almost impassable; but that
cry only showed the injustice of blaming individuals for occurrences over which they had no control. From want of a system of sufficient land-
carriage, the horses belonging to the cavalry had
to struggle up to their knees in mud, under
burdens of provision for the army. The want of
that land-carriage is admitted, I believe, on all
hands to have been the principal cause of the
misfortunes of the army, and it, therefore, well
deserves the consideration of this House." * * * *

CHAPTER XIII.

THE EFFECTS OF THE PUBLIC PRESS ON THE WAR.

" If I'm traduced by tongues, which neither know
  My faculties, nor person, yet will be
  The chroniclers of my doing,—let me say
  'T is but the fate of place, and the rough brake
  That virtue must go through.   We must not stint
  Our necessary actions, in the fear
  To cope malicious censurers "—

To the great anxieties incidental to Lord Raglan's
position, anxieties in council as well as in the field,
were thus added those occasioned by the extreme
suffering of his troops during the winter.   While his
thoughts were constantly directed to the amelioration
of their condition, and while the chiefs of the various
administrative departments under him were employed
in the unceasing endeavour to carry out his orders in
these respects, the English press, more especially the
Times newspaper, suddenly commenced attacking
Lord Raglan's character and conduct in the most
unjustifiable and unmeasured language; imputing to
his incapacity and want of foresight the failure of the
siege, and the lamentable position of the army.

Imperfectly acquainted with the real facts; ignoring the previous want of preparation; forgetting that the expedition had been undertaken greatly in consequence of the strenuous advocacy of the press itself; now that results had not answered the expectations formed, Lord Raglan and his staff were selected as the victims for popular indignation.

The following are specimens of the violent language constantly made use of at the time :—

"The army has been sacrificed to the grossest mismanagement. Incompetency, lethargy, aristocratic hauteur, official indifference, favour, routine, perverseness, and stupidity reign, revel, and riot in the camp before Sebastopol, in Balaclava, and at Scutari."

Again we read :—"Send out men who will save the army, not from the Russians, but from despair. Reinforcements march to their graves, and begin to perish by scores, from the hour they land. Misrule receives them on the beach, wearies them, worries them, drenches them, shivers them, and so destroys them, till a few spectral figures are all that remain." And so on, day after day.

Was such language justifiable? Was it a credit to a country professing a love of justice? And still further, was it true in its inferences? Surely not. Surely it is now perfectly clear and understood, that the failure of the first attempt on Sebastopol, and the consequent sufferings of the British army in the winter of 1854, arose from causes far different to what are inferred in the above words.

The people of England, with feelings deeply affected at the time by the threatened extinction of their army, and in a great measure ignorant of the real causes of the disaster, adopted, to a certain degree, the language and the sentiments of the press ; so that Lord Raglan, who but a short time before had been universally spoken of as having displayed great judgment, enterprise, and talent, strategic skill, military daring, and the calmest courage, who, in fact, had shown himself possessed of all the attributes of a great general and a hero, was suddenly represented as a poor, feeble old man, incapable of mental exertion, ignorant of the condition of his army, careless of their fate, and never visible beyond the door of his house.

There was great inconsistency on the very face of such an abrupt change of opinion. The character of a man does not descend thus rapidly from the skilful and heroic, to the feeble and incompetent. But there was a still greater injustice and want of fair play in this hasty condemnation of Lord Raglan and his staff, solely upon the one-sided testimony of irresponsible and anonymous authorities. But—

> *   *   *   *   *   "Applause
> Waits on success; the fickle multitude,
> Like the light straw that floats along the stream,
> Glide with the current still, and follow fortune."

The well-known character of Lord Raglan, his extreme kindness of heart and gentleness of disposition, ought to have been sufficient to protect him from the assertion that he was indifferent to the sufferings of his army. With respect to the charge brought against him, of not visiting the camps during the winter of 1854, it is not, of course, easy to collect direct evidence to rebut so unexpected a libel. But an officer of his own staff fortunately kept a record to a certain extent of Lord Raglan's movements during that period, and in a work entitled " Realities of the late War, by a Staff Officer," has given a complete contradiction to this venemous untruth.

The following extract from the manly speech of the Earl of Winchelsea made in the House of Lords at the time is true and to the point.

Speaking of Lord Raglan, he says :—

" What has the Times stated of that noble lord ? Why, that he had no feeling, no sympathy in the sufferings and privations of the gallant men he commanded ; that he never was seen in camp and among his men. A more foul, false, and malignant calumny never was levelled against the character of any man on earth ; for if there be one man on earth, more than another, who possesses a really kind heart and sympathy with those placed under him, it is the noble lord who commands our army in the Crimea."

Owing to the injurious aspersions on his character, Lord Raglan was deprived of the confidence of the people of England at a moment when he most required support, and the consequences might have been still more serious, had not the excellent spirit and discipline of the troops under his command prevented them from receiving and adopting the spirit of the press.

Great and undoubted as are the advantages of a free expression of public opinion under ordinary circumstances, it should be borne in mind that a time of war is for a nation one of difficulty and one of danger. The utmost confidence should therefore be placed in, and the greatest forbearance shown towards, those in high command, to support them in their arduous and responsible position. However great the energies of a man may be, however elevated his character, the knowledge that at a critical moment his most heroic acts and his most honest intentions are liable to be misrepresented, and held up to public ridicule and odium, must tend to render his position still more difficult and embarrassed. Further, as the success of a general depends to a certain extent upon the confidence of the troops in their commander, the constant public depreciation of his talents goes far to deprive him of this prestige of victory, and might lead to dangerous disaffection amongst those under his command.

I am aware that these opinions are opposed to those of many persons in England, who consider that the utmost latitude of expression should be allowed in all public matters ; but leaving this part of the question for the moment, at all events it cannot be questioned that Lord Raglan, as chief of an army in the field, on whom at the time the attention, not only of England, but of Europe was fixed, had a right to expect entire support and confidence from the English Government.

The proper course of the Ministry was perfectly clear. If Lord Raglan were, as stated, incompetent and unfit, he should have been recalled ; if otherwise, and if he was to be retained at his post, it became the bounden duty of Ministers to render his position as little difficult as possible, and to take every opportunity, by constant explanation, to defend him, and to dissipate the false impressions produced by the ever-continued attacks of the public journals.

But such a course was not adopted. Lord Raglan was not recalled, but neither was he defended. No voice was raised on his behalf. Lord Panmure, on coming into office as Minister for War, at a time when the feelings of the country were deeply moved on the subject, was significantly silent as regarded Lord Raglan. With respect to the officers of the staff in the Crimea, the Minister for War at once showed that he had arrived at a foregone conclusion. In the House of Lords he stated openly his regret that the Adjutant and Quarter-Master-General's department were not supposed to be competent.

By whom was this supposed? Had Lord Raglan thus reported of his staff? It is perfectly well known that the contrary was the case. But the nation was angry, the Minister subservient; so leaving Lord Raglan to his fate, he threw the blame upon the chief officers of the staff, and endeavoured to recall them. Lord Raglan resisted this unworthy attempt, not only as a matter of justice to the individuals concerned, but because he felt that their removal at such a time would be a great public injury.

Lord Panmure then despatched General Simpson to the seat of war, to report upon these departments. The report of this officer afterwards was as follows :— " Ever since my arrival in the camp, it has been my daily custom, by personal intercourse, to make myself acquainted with every officer employed on the general staff of this army, and there is not one of them I would wish to see removed. I confess myself to have come among those officers with some degree of prejudice against them in my mind, by the gross misrepresentations current in England respecting them. I do not think a better selection of staff officers could be made."

It would appear, therefore, that the Minister for War was quite mistaken in his estimate of the efficiency of the staff. But independently of the injustice to individuals, in thus hastily imputing the misfortunes of the army to their incapacity, the evil is still greater in a public point of view. The true lesson, that is, in time of peace to prepare for war, is apt to be lost sight of, and there is consequently no guarantee that such disasters may not recur; or that a nation, which proved itself so little ready for purposes of attack, may not some day find herself equally unprepared for purposes of defence.

Whatever differences of opinion may exist, as to the advantages or otherwise of unlimited criticism upon the character and abilities of a general officer commanding an army in the field, the necessity of great caution in publishing communications respecting the movements of the army, its strength and preparations, hardly requires an argument.

In war, secrecy is one of the elements of success. Of the practicability of maintaining it, even in the present day, and of the consequent advantages, sufficient proofs were given during the late war, in the acknowledged facts, that previously to the landing of the allies, no reliable information could be obtained, either of the numerical force of the Russians in the Crimea, or of the actual condition of the land defences of Sebastopol.   But a still more striking evidence of the secrecy of the Russian plans was afforded by the circumstance, that for some time after our arrival it was universally supposed that there were only two roads of communication between the Crimea and the main-land ; the one by Perekop, and the other by the spit of Arabat ; whereas, it was subsequently ascertained, that a third, and to us an unknown road, had for some time existed between the two points named, across the shallow waters of the Putrid Sea.   In fact, the great advantages of secrecy were fully appreciated in every respect by the enemy, and throughout the war the greatest difficulties were experienced by the allies in obtaining accurate information.

The English nation, on the contrary, having commenced the war with a small army, totally unprepared for active operations, at the same time disdained taking any precautions to prevent their weakness or deficiencies being perfectly known in all their details to the enemy. Correspondents from the principal newspapers accompanied the army everywhere, and their presence was legitimized and acknowledged by the Government, so far that they were allowed rations, forage, and transport. These gentlemen, many of them talented and accomplished men, made it their occupation, openly and unreservedly, to ascertain the strength of the army, its condition, and state of preparation ; and, by constant and minute observation, were enabled to foreshadow the probable plans and movements of the allied generals. That their opinions and prophecies should frequently prove correct, can hardly be matter of wonder. They were acquainted with many officers of the army, and had every opportunity of gaining most valuable information, which was immediately sent to England and published in the daily papers. Thus, no sooner had the allied generals decided upon the expedition to the Crimea, than it was made known, and the very place of landing pointed out. When the army arrived before Sebastopol, the number and calibre of our guns in the batteries, the situation of our magazines, the weak points of our position, the number of our sick, our difficulties in transport, want of ammunition, and a thousand other daily details of our progress, were all chronicled with a clearness and precision, gratifying, possibly, as a proof of the intelligence of the gentlemen in question, highly interesting to the public, but at the same time of a most fatal and damaging influence as regards the success of the general cause ; inasmuch as these accounts were equally open to, and taken instant advantage of, by our enemies.

On this point Lord Winchelsea at the time spoke, and spoke truly, as follows :—

" My opinion is, that if a spy were in our camp, paid by all the gold with which the enemy could reward him, he could not give them more useful information, or more detrimental to the interests of our army, than the correspondent of the Times newspaper has afforded them. Would the Duke of Wellington have suffered such a state of things, in any army which he ever had the command of ? Would he have allowed the weaknesses and the losses of our army, the diminution of our forces, their sickness, our loss of cavalry, and other losses, to be detailed for the information of the enemy, so as to place our army in a still more fearful situation than that in which it is now placed ? "

In consequence of the serious mischief resulting from the suicidal course of the English press, Lord Raglan, in the month of December, 1854, wrote to the Minister for War, representing the injurious effect of thus conveying intelligence to the enemy, and giving an instance in which the objects of the allies had been thwarted, and those of the enemy assisted, by a communication in a newspaper.

The steps taken by the Duke of Newcastle are thus related in a speech made in the House of Lords :—

" Upon receiving this communication I took a step

which I believe a Minister of the Crown is not justi-
fied in taking, unless in very extreme cases indeed.
I addressed myself to the newspaper press of London,
requesting they would abstain from publishing such
intelligence as might be useful to the enemy, and so
prejudicial to the operations of our own army. It
was the first time I ever made such an application,
and I should not have done so, feeling the impossibility of attempting to interfere peremptorily, if I had
not absolutely felt it my duty to interpose in a friendly
spirit, to endeavour to obtain so great an object.

" As I said before, I wrote to the editors of the
London press, stating the nature of the complaints
made by Lord Raglan, pointing out the inconvenience
which had arisen, and appealing to their patriotism
and sense of duty to exercise a vigilant control over
communications, not only from their own correspondents, but over the private letters received by them,
which are in many instances doubtless as mischievous,
if not more so, than the letters of newspaper correspondents ; and urgently requesting them to put a stop to
the mischief, which resulted from such publication.
From some of the conductors of journals thus
addressed, I received no answers, but those I did receive were of a most courteous description, promising
that the greatest care should be taken for the future.

" I can only say, I do regret that the courteous
promises contained in those letters have not been as
completely and as thoroughly fulfilled as, I must say,
I had reason to expect ; for Lord Raglan has had

occasion to make another complaint, which I received only the day before yesterday, pointing out reports of the same character, proceeding from the same quarter, on the 18th of December.

" I deeply deplore these facts, but it will not be my duty to make a similar communication again, and I can only regret that my first communication has not been so successful as I had reason—on the part of the public, and not in any way on my own account—to anticipate." * * * *

The following singular leading article is the reply of the Times newspaper to the protest of the War Minister.

" Strong objections have been expressed in quarters that claim our highest respect, to the free publication of letters from the East, containing news likely to be serviceable to the enemy. That we have gone to the verge of prudence, in satisfying the curiosity, or the scientific interest, of our readers, we cannot deny ; and on a cursory perusal of our columns, it might seem at first sight that we had conveyed a dangerous amount of information. We have described the positions of the camps, of the different divisions, and of the head quarters ; the number of the guns mounted in the several batteries, the unexpected and untoward diminution of our forces by disease, the difficulty of getting up ammunition, the roads, and the various speculations afloat as to the manner and success of the siege. We have even remarked on the fact, that the distinguishing uniforms of officers had drawn upon

themselves, and particularly on the staff, the fire of
the enemy.   More we have told that might seem of
a dangerous character.   We say, we have told all this,
but the fact is, the letters of private correspondents
contain quite as much detail, and in some instances
more detail, of a military character, than the more
picturesque descriptions of our own correspondent.
Moreover, it is not only we, but the whole newspaper
press, that has done the same; and if we have given
fuller and more particular information, it is only in
accordance with our usual habit.

" But the newspapers have not done more, nay, in
our opinion, not nearly so much as the map-sellers,
who have done their best to ascertain and publish the
disposition of the besieging forces, with an exactness
impossible to the pen.   Indeed, when every mail from
the East brings many thousand letters; when not only
every subaltern pretends to be a tactician, but every
corporal has his budget of military gossip; and when
there are several hundred newspapers in this country,
ready to pick up every stray scrap of information that
they can call their own; it is evident that the evil
complained of is gigantic; that is, it is commensurate
with the whole British public and the people.   In
fact, it is nothing more or less than that publicity
which is the life, not only of freedom, but equally of
all political action, in this country.   It is not this
journal or that, or all the journals, or the whole litera-
ture of England, but the very atmosphere in which

we live, and which with all its advantages may now and then have a drawback, or seem to have one.

" In the first place, we candidly admit that it is possible for information from the seat of war to be too full and particular; needlessly so for the interest of the general reader, and of real use to the enemy only. We have seen private letters that we should certainly have hesitated to publish. Of our own accord, we have struck out passages from the correspondence in our hands for publication, even when the writer had already observed as much abstinence as he thought of any use.

" A contemporary has published the exact position of the mines prepared by the besiegers, and that information has actually led to countermines; and consequently to the sacrifice of the labour in those mines, thus discovered to the enemy. We have rigorously abstained from giving any hints of this sort. Indeed, we have ever had in our eye the fact, that there are Russian agents and partisans in this country, who peruse the newspapers every morning, in quest of hints for their employers; and who, by means of the telegraph, can communicate what they may think of any service, to Berlin, and thence to Warsaw, before the Times is in the hands of the London reader.

" We are too well aware of the fact, that during the whole of the war, the shortest road from Sebastopol to London, and consequently from London to Sebastopol, has been through St. Petersburgh.

Without any undue presumption, we think we may claim to have almost invariably avoided even the appearance of needless disclosure in the character of our information. Some of the earlier letters of our correspondent necessarily referred to the disposition of our army; but subsequently, they have been narratives of actions and other incidents, such as a spectator on both sides might have written.

" In a battle both sides are so near and intermixed, that nothing can be seen by one, which is not equally conspicuous to the other; and it will be found accordingly, that we have given as full and exact accounts of the Russian troops and their movements, as we have of our own. By the same rule, we believe the Russian generals at Sebastopol could give quite as full an account of the several engagements as they could find in these columns.

" The most serious charge that could be brought against the press, is, that in aiming at the picturesque, or in bringing the scene more minutely before the eye of the reader, it has called attention to the distinguishing uniforms of the officers, and so led to their very great comparative loss in action. That this loss has been so greatly beyond all proportion to that of the rank and file as to excite painful inquiry, we admit with much concern. But there is, and there always has been, this disproportionate loss of officers in

the British army, whenever the mode of warfare
at all admitted of it. It was so in the American
war. It has been so whenever there was a rifle
or a marksman in the ranks of the enemy. It
will continue to be so, as long as we choose to
continue the absurdity of dressing up our officers
so conspicuously, that they may be distinguished
a mile off. The loss of officers' was quite as
great at the Alma, as at Balaclava or Inkermann.
Indeed, for years past, long before Russia broke
loose over Europe, the question of officers' uniforms has been discussed in these columns, and
numerous instances have been cited, to show that
officers paid for their finery on parade a double
chance of casualties in war. What has happened
then in the Crimea, is only what we have always
pointed out, as it now appears, to little purpose.
If officers must wear cocked hats and white
plumes; if they must be dressed in blue, while
the common soldiers are dressed in scarlet; and
if they must be on horseback among their infantry, let no one throw on the press at home
the blame of their speedy recognition. In the last
terrible action many of the men had their great
coats on, and therefore formed a still stronger foil
to the brilliancy of the officers and staff. In fact,
the necessities of war are in this country most
cruelly sacrificed to the caprices of peace. We
dress our officers for parade, we give them up to
royal tailors who never smelt powder except in

a preserve or a field day at Woolwich. As to
the supposition that the Russian marksmen were
at first disposed to overlook the men with cocked
hats and white plumes, supposing them to be
merely the Commissariat, we believe that to be
entirely a mistake; for we cannot conceive the
commonest soldier, or the merest savage in the
Russian army, to make so absurd and gratuitous a
blunder.

" But even if publicity should have seemed to
serve the cause of the enemy in one or two instances, that is not worth mention compared to
the immense service rendered to the army by
bringing the force of public opinion to bear on
the authorities at home. Would reinforcements and
supplies have been sent so promptly and so
abundantly, and in so many new kinds, but for
the public exposure of the state of things in the
army?

" It may hurt the pride and try the temper
of our rulers, to have the sufferings and peril of
our army in the Crimea made known to their
countrymen. We might attempt to deceive the
enemy and gratify our own conceit, by drawing a
flourishing account of whole legions living comfort-
ably in warm weather-proof habitations; enjoying
the luxury of a good larder, a good kitchen, and
a healthy digestion. We might describe fabulous
guns, with inexhaustible magazines, mysteriously
situated beyond the reach of hostile shells. We

might so represent the state of our troops, that on the day of disaster there would be the verdict that it was nobody's fault, and no account could be given of it, except the visitation of God. But it is quite clear such a course would be treason to our country, and, we should think, the greatest unkindness to the army and its officers. Vain would be their most urgent applications for assistance, were they not backed by the voice of public opinion at home. Ministers and functionaries of every degree would sit and talk, or reckon the cost, and demur, and delay, and do nothing, until all was over, and nothing remained but to gloss over the consequences of procrastination. At this moment everything is being done that a great nation can do ; but in how many instances would nothing have been done at all, but for the terrible light which the press has thrown upon every stage of the expedition ?

" While we admit the propriety of great reserve as to information which may possibly be of use to the enemy, and while we declare our intention of maintaining that reserve, we beg that our services may not be forgotten, and that we may still be permitted to tender those services, by making known at home, from time to time, the true state of the allied armies and their heroic deeds."

There is much false reasoning, and there are many transparent fallacies, contained in the above curious and apologetic article, some of which deserve a momentary consideration.

1. The argument that private letters were even more explicit than those of the regular correspondents is merely an additional reason for caution in publishing them.

2. As to the map-sellers, who are considered by the Times as even more capable of evil in the matter of publicity than the public journals, it need only be remarked, that however accurate plans might be, they still could not be forwarded by telegraph; and as their preparation occupied some time, the information they contained was not so recent, and therefore not so valuable to the enemy.

3. Again,—although publicity may be the life of freedom and of political action in England, the present is not a political question, but one simply relating to military operations. There is a time for all things, and discretion is sometimes necessary. A man who might innocently light a fire in the middle of a desert plain, would be insane to do so in a powder magazine.

4. The Times acknowledges that a contemporary has published the position of the besiegers' mines, which has led to countermines, and states that they " have rigorously abstained from giving any hints of this sort." This assertion was published on the 7th of December, 1854. It is, therefore, somewhat remarkable to find in the columns of the Times of the 26th of January, 1855, a paragraph as follows :—

" From our correspondent at Marseilles.—Letters from the Crimea of the 12th state, the Flagstaff battery had been mined by the French, who only waited for a favourable opportunity to blow it up."

And it is still more remarkable to read the following despatch from Prince Menschikoff, dated 12th of February, 1855.

"On the 30th (of January) we succeeded in discovering subterraneous works of the French, leading towards the fortifications ; with the aid of artillery we destroyed, on the 2nd, a portion of the enemy's gallery, &c. &c.

The one announcement certainly reads like a sequence to the other.

5. That part of the article which relates to the distinguishing uniforms of the officers bears no real relation to the question at issue. The dress of the British army is no secret, and coloured representations of the various grades can be bought at any time for a few shillings in the London print shops.

6. The article, towards the close, changes its ground of argument, and asserts that all needless disclosures have been avoided. The columns of the Times throughout the war will give frequent instances that such discretion was soon laid on one side ; but one example will suffice. On the 12th of February, 1855, amongst a variety of other details, the Sebastopol correspondent states :—" We have a fine battery ready to open on the steamer which is anchored towards the head of the creek near Inkermann, and which has caused us so much annoyance by her shells."

13

There is much truth in all that is urged as to the power and beneficial influence of the press upon the Government ; but it would not appear impossible to exercise this influence, even during a period of war, and at the same time to avoid entering into such details as give a dangerous amount of information to the enemy.

Our allies have both given their opinions on the duties of the press during war.

The Moniteur says,—" It is useful to remind the press, both in France and abroad, of the imperious duties of discretion which the security and interest of our troops impose on their patriotism and impartiality. For the purpose of gratifying the impatience (otherwise so legitimate) of their readers, the journals publish, on the military operations of the Crimea, information sometimes correct, but more frequently false, which is transmitted to them from the theatre of war, or taken from letters written by officers and soldiers to their families. When these recitals are false, they mislead public opinion ; and when true, are attended with a still more serious inconvenience,—that of giving the enemy some idea of the plans and means of attack combined by the Generals-in-chief in their secret councils ; and so everything that ought carefully to be kept secret is revealed. In both cases this publicity is dangerous and even culpable. Again, to change these confidential letters into articles for journals, is to expose the lives of the heroic besiegers.

In time of war, silence is sometimes a sacred duty for those who every day address the public ; if journals lose something by this, as far as their interest goes, they gain considerably in self-respect."

General La Marmora's order on the same subject is as follows :—

GENERAL ORDER ISSUED TO THE SARDINIAN ARMY.— " Kadikoi, September 16th.—The correspondence of the military and of the civilians attached to the expeditionary corps, with the journals, is highly objectionable ; it describes the operations, precise positions, the forces, and preparations of every kind ; it is prejudicial, inasmuch as it informs the enemy of what we desire he should not know.   If correspondents discuss what may have happened, or what may have been done, they fall into criticism which is against discipline, and such an abuse cannot be tolerated in a well-organized army ; if they speak of the armies of our allies, they give rise to recriminations, and disturb the harmony without which it is impossible the alliance can bear its fruits.   If, to avoid the evils I have above mentioned, they contain merely ambiguous statements, that, from want of positive information, forms but an incomplete and incorrect correspondence which does but small credit to the military and civil branches of the army from which they proceed.   For these reasons, I think it right to warn military and civilians belonging to the expeditionary corps, and also naval division, that I will

13 *

severely punish the authors of a correspondence which may fall within the categories above pointed out.— ALPHONSE DE LA MARMORA."

The Articles of War of the British army are also very distinct on the subject of affording information to the enemy. As follows :—

" Any officer or soldier who shall hold correspondence with, or give intelligence to, the enemy, directly or indirectly, shall on conviction of any one of the aforesaid offences, suffer DEATH, penal servitude for a term of not less than four years, or such other punishment as by a general court-martial shall be awarded.

In a time of war, civilians and all others following an army are subject to martial law.

CHAPTER XIV.

This volume closes at a period when, the first attempt upon Sebastopol having failed, the allied armies found themselves suddenly overtaken by winter, with open trenches before the place ; at the same time that, from want of means, they were unable to continue offensive operations, and they remained thus for some months, hemmed in by the Russians in a corner of the Crimea.

In the opening chapter of the work I endeavoured to explain that the army of England, on the breaking out of war, was few in numbers, and that, small even as it was, it was unprovided with the establishments necessary for an army in the field. Every movement that it made, and every action in which it was engaged, betrayed its weakness in these respects ; and this want of preparation not only added greatly to the difficulties of Lord Raglan's position, but prevented him from being able to take proper advantage of the victories which the valour of his troops gained for him.

Had the campaign been an ordinary one, all these defects would have become rapidly apparent; but the
army having been ordered, in spite of its defective
establishments, and in spite of the sickness at Varna
which decimated its ranks, to proceed on an expedition at a late season, and to undertake, with means
entirely inadequate, the capture of a stronghold possessing unlimited resources, and which latter had been
collecting for years; under these circumstances its
defects became still more glaring, and cause and effect
rapidly followed each other, so much so that, before the
campaign had lasted two months, the army was not
only struggling against overwhelming numbers for
the very ground on which it stood; but so perfectly
destitute was it of the commonest necessaries, of
clothing, food, shelter, &c., that it was threatened with
absolute extinction from natural causes, independently
of any enemy whatever.

I have endeavoured to show that this state of affairs
was in no way attributable to Lord Raglan, or to
those under him; on the contrary, that, by valour,
skill, and daring in the field, and by incessant activity
and thought in council, they endeavoured, as far as lay
in their power, to overcome difficulties and to mitigate
disasters. That they could not prevent a very dis-
tressing state of affairs, was simply because it was not
in the power of any man to remedy on the spot the previous national neglect of years. All the wealth of
England, so much of which was recklessly spent after-

wards, could not then have saved the army from intense suffering, or the nation from reproach.

With regard to the influence of the public press on the war, I have endeavoured to show in the first place, that in imputing the difficulties and the misfortunes of the army to Lord Raglan and his staff, it entirely misled the nation; and not only thus was great injustice done to individuals, but the true lesson which England ought to learn is apt to be lost sight of.

In the second place, that the press, by its gross calumnies of Lord Raglan and the higher officers, might have produced dangerous disaffection in the ranks of the army, had not the excellent discipline of the latter fortunately been proof to such evil influences.

In the third place, as regards the press, I have endeavoured to show, that by publishing indiscriminately every detail of military operations, it almost rendered it impossible to conduct those operations to a successful issue.

In a time of peace, free discussions on all public matters are of incalculable value, as regards the national welfare; and such discussions are, in fact, a vital part of the English constitution; but in a time of war, discretion on some subjects becomes equally a duty, in which latter, therefore, the public press at the time appears to have failed.

These remarks may be unpopular, but they are true, and it is most important that the causes of our misfortunes should be accurately understood, so as, if possible, to prevent a recurrence of them ; and it is a matter of simple justice to those officers who have been so cruelly maligned and held up to public indignation for supposed incompetency, that the truth should be made manifest, and that they should receive from the nation the acquittal they deserve.

The next volume will give an account of the series of extraordinary battles which ensued in front of Sebastopol, during the first nine months of the year 1855.*

The exhaustion of the allies during the previous winter had afforded time to the Russians to enclose their city within a chain of strong earth-works, with a deep ditch along the whole fron . The Russians also constructed numerous bomb-proofs in all the principal works, sufficient to shelter a large garrison from the heavy fire which they no doubt felt would eventually be poured upon them. Their almost unlimited supply of guns of heavy calibre enabled them to arm batteries which swept the approaches in every direction. By great exertions, they also succeeded in assembling a very large force of infantry drawn from distant parts of the empire; so that when the allies once more renewed the attack in the following spring, they still proved too weak to overcome these concentrated means of resistance, and again and again found

* Since this paragraph was penned, circumstances have occurred to prevent the author from carrying the narrative any further for the present. (*Vide Preface.*)

their own resources exhausted, and their gallantry apparently unavailing.   Months thus passed away and the struggle appeared almost interminable.

The army of England had incurred such severe losses in the winter of 1854, and the reserves at home were so limited, that it never regained its pristine strength.   The country had only recruits to send out to stand in the place of those trained and highly disciplined men, whose conduct in the earlier battles of the war added so brilliant a chapter to the history of the English army.

The French, on the other hand, with vast reserves at home, increased their numbers almost at will, and therefore gradually exercised, not only in the field, but in the council, a predominant influence in the progress of the struggle.

With regard to General Canrobert, who commanded them for some months, brave as he was in action, and magnanimous as he proved himself to be in resigning his high appointment, still there is no doubt that his indecision on several critical occasions, when unswerving resolution alone could have led to success, tended to prolong the siege, and postponed that consummation which his eager magnificent army so ardently longed for.

The sad death of that great man Field-Marshal Lord Raglan removed the greatest spirit from the scene of contest.   Little appreciated as he was at the time by his countrymen at home, still his army ever loved him; and the generals of the allied powers soon betrayed, by their distracted councils, that he whose charm of manner had so often successfully softened the asperities of jarring interests, whose simple and great character had won their esteem, and whose valour, rivalling that of the heroes of antiquity, had gained their admiration—was gone from among them.

Fortunately for the allies, a man, who, although of a totally different stamp, still possessed the peculiar qualities so much wanted at the time to overcome the great difficulties of the position, had already been found in the ranks of the French army, and when General Pelissier succeeded to the chief command, from that day the fate of Sebastopol was sealed.

Rough in his manner, and rude in his language, disdaining to use any arts to soften differences, or to conciliate opinions, it at once became apparent that, whether success or otherwise should be the final result, at all events no hesitation or change of plan should mark his course. Rejecting the varied advice which had so constantly perplexed his predecessor; stedfastly refusing to adopt plans, or to be guided by the opinion, of others at a distance, however high their rank, General Pelissier boldly proclaimed to the astonished generals of the French army, that so long as he were at its head, his word should be law, and his will unquestioned. He told them plainly, that distinguished and skilful as they were, he wanted not their advice; and that they were but tools to carry out his great views.

Gradually, as the allies increased in numbers, and

as their concentrated resources gave them the superiority, he tightened the network which hemmed in the devoted city ; until at length, on the 8th of September, 1856, at his signal, the allied armies rushed to the assault, and General Pelissier planted his heel on the ruins of the Malakoff. With upwards of 20,000 wounded combatants stretched upon the ground, with its fleet sunk, its arsenal captured, midst the roar of successive explosions, drenched in human blood, and blackened with fire, so Sebastopol fell, and they worthily named the conqueror—Pelissier, Duke of Malakoff.

THE END.

JOHN CHILDS AND SON, PRINTERS.